THE VIRTUES
OF THE PROPHET

A YOUNG MUSLIM'S GUIDE
TO THE GREATER JIHAD,
THE WAR AGAINST
THE PASSIONS

CHARLES UPTON

THE VIRTUES
OF THE PROPHET

A YOUNG MUSLIM'S GUIDE
TO THE GREATER JIHAD,
THE WAR AGAINST
THE PASSIONS

WITH *TAFSIR* OF
THE HOLY QU'RAN

SOPHIA PERENNIS

SAN RAFAEL, CA

First published in the USA
by Sophia Perennis
© Charles Upton 2006

Series editor: James R. Wetmore

For information, address:
Sophia Perennis, P.O. Box 151011
San Rafael, CA 94915
sophiaperennis.com

Library of Congress Cataloging-in-Publication Data

Upton, Charles, 1948–
The virtues of the Prophet: a young muslim's guide to the
greater jihad, the war against the passions:
with tafsir of the holy Qur'an/
Charles Upton.—1ˢᵗ ed.

p. cm.
ISBN 1 59731 051 4 (pbk: alk. paper)
ISBN 1 59731 052 2 (hardcover: alk. paper)
1. Muhammad, Prophet, d. 632—Devotional literature.
2. Muhammad, Prophet, d. 632—Ethics.
3. Muhammad, Prophet, d. 632—Appreciation.
4. Muhammad, Prophet, d. 632, in the Koran. I. Title
BP76.2.U67   2006
297.6'3—dc22   2006021556

ACKNOWLEDGMENTS

Some sections of this book appeared in *The Book of Character, Writings on Virtue from Islamic and Other Sources* by Camille Helminski, and *The Book of Revelations, Selections and Interpretations of the Holy Qur'an*, Kabir Helminski, editor; reprinted with the kind permission of The Book Foundation, UK.

Selections from *Islam and the Destiny of Man* by Charles Le Gai Eaton are reprinted by permission of the Islamic Texts Society, the holder of the copyright.

The quotations from *A Return to Modesty: Discovering the Hidden Virtue*, copyright 1999 by Wendy Shalit, are reprinted with the permission of The Free Press, a division of Simon & Schuster Adult Publishing Group.

Passages from *The Makkan Crucible and Sunshine at Madinah* by Zakaria Bashier are reprinted with the permission of The Islamic Foundation, Leicester, UK.

CONTENTS

INTRODUCTION:
THE GREATER *JIHAD*

Once when the Prophet Muhammad, peace and blessings upon him, was returning from battle, he told his companions: 'Now we are returning from the lesser jihad to the greater jihad.' 'And what is the greater jihad?' they asked. The Prophet answered: 'The struggle against the self.'

— Prophetic Hadith

IT HAS BEEN SAID THAT 'Islam is the meeting between God as such and man as such.' For the nature of God, we have the first part of the *shahada*: 'I testify that there is no god but God.' For the nature of man—for there can be no conception of Who God is without a corresponding idea of what man is—we have the second half: 'And I testify that Muhammad is God's Prophet.' For Islam, the door to the true nature of man is the character of Muhammad, peace and blessings be upon him. He is the Complete Man, *al-Insan al-Kamil*. He is the exemplar of our *fitrah*, of the human form in its original nature as God created it. The love Muslims feel for the person of the Prophet has to do with the fullness of his humanity—not in any sentimental sense, but rather because in him is revealed an unfailing and providential capacity to bring out the full humanity of any and every situation, and then act upon it. *Whichever way you turn, there is the face of God* says the Qur'an. But it would be almost equally true to say, 'Whichever way you turn, there is the example of the Prophet.'

Muslims love Muhammad and model themselves upon him ... this love is central in the spiritual life of Islam, lending to an otherwise austere religion something that is at once passionate and gentle. He is loved for his courage and for his tenderness, not only as a warrior and a master of men, but also as a perfect father, a perfect husband and a perfect friend—and the humblest, most wretched man or woman, thinking of him, will dream of having such a friend. Those who were closest to him were known, not as 'disciples' but as 'companions'; almost fourteen centuries after his death, it is in this companionship that the Muslim finds comfort in loneliness and courage in adversity, and this world would be a cold and inhospitable place without him.

'No one,' wrote Constance Padwick, a Christian caught in the net of this love, 'can estimate the power of Islam as a religion who does not take into account the love at heart of it for this figure. It is here that human emotion, repressed at some points by the austerity of the doctrine of God as developed in theology, has its full outlet—a warm human emotion which the peasant can share with the mystic. The love of this figure is perhaps the strongest binding force in a religion which has so marked a binding power.'

To love Muhammad is one thing, but to imitate him—to try to be 'like' him—is another. He was the last messenger and the last prophet, so how can we expect to imitate what is by definition unique and unrepeatable? In the first place his virtues are to be imitated, and they were providentially exemplified in the extraordinary variety of human experience through which he passed in his sixty-two years of life. He was an orphan, yet he knew the warmth of parental love through his grandfather's devoted care for him; he was a faithful husband of one wife for many years, and after her death, the tender and considerate husband of many wives; he was the father of children who gave him the greatest joy this world has to offer, and he saw all but one of them die; he had been a shepherd and a merchant when young, and he became a ruler, a statesman, a military commander, and a law-giver; he loved his native city and was driven from it in exile, finally to return home in triumph and set an example of clemency which has no equal in human history.[1]

---

1. Charles Le Gai Eaton, *Islam and the Destiny of Man* (Albany, NY: State University of New York Press, 1985), pp 65–66.

The essence of the Islamic view of humanity, which is both the ideal we strive for and the norm according to which we are created, is *unity of character*—a unity that is indistinguishable from beauty. Whatever is unified is balanced. Whatever is balanced is well-proportioned. Whatever is well-proportioned is beautiful. The beauty of the Prophet's character does not lie in an overwhelming brilliance, or a blunt forcefulness, or a beguiling fascination, or a terrifying majesty. The character of the Prophet equally reflects all the Names of God, with no one Name predominating. It is this specific beauty, a beauty based on balance and unity, which makes him the norm and exemplar of the human state.

In a unified character, thought, feeling, and action form a single whole. No one faculty is sacrificed or suppressed in the name of the others, or becomes overcharged and inflated so that it lives at the expense of the others. Insofar as we are *will*, we submit to God, and deal justly with things, persons and situations. Insofar as we are *feelings*, we love God and our neighbor. Insofar as we are *intelligence*, we know God, and know creation in the light of God. All three are equally part of what we are, and all three appear, in a perfect synthesis, in the character of Muhammad. The Prophet was powerful and decisive in action, sometimes harshly rigorous in his pursuit of justice, as well as balanced and restrained—but he was not, in the Western sense, a 'man of action', a kind of Arab Napoleon. The Prophet was affectionate to companions and family and merciful to enemies and to the needy and oppressed, but he was neither a 'sentimentalist' nor a 'philanthropist'. The Prophet was highly intelligent on both the spiritual and the social planes of reality, but he was not a 'genius'. He was, precisely, a man. If we look for spiritual exaltation in this man, we will find it. If we look for the more humble and ordinary aspects of human life, there they are. If we look for awe and trembling in the face of the terrible Majesty of God, these too are in evidence. What we do not find, try as we may, are imbalance, or irresponsibility, or obsession, or tyranny, or cowardice, or betrayal of trust, or betrayal of self. This perfect adequacy of the Prophet's nature to every perspective from which we view it, this lack of imbalance between the sublime and the mundane in his character, is the reflection in him of the Islamic doctrine that each Name of God contains all the others. Some Names are incomparably sublime, others apparently less so—but all are Names of the One God, the One Essence.

In the Islamic view, humanity is both *'abd*, God's slave, and *khalifa*, God's fully-empowered representative in this world. This is our *fitrah*. And our central example of what it is to be *'abd* and *khalifa* is Muhammad. He is submission to God was perfect, not because, like some of the greatest saints, he intensely desired to submit to God in a passionate and self-sacrificial way, but because he was one with the nature of things—and according to the nature of things, in the face of the Absolute Reality of God, the creature is as nothing. Whatever reality he has is a pure gift from the Absolute Reality, nor can he ever break out of, or wander away from, the sovereign Will of God. Whether or not he submits *willingly*, he always submits *actually*. Muhammad knew this, and therefore submitted willingly, and perfectly.

> Not only does the messenger who is a slave subordinate his own will to that of his Lord; there is nothing in his mind or in his memory that could obstruct the free passage of revelation. Muhammad is *'abd* and *rasul*; he is also *nabi al-ummi*, the unlettered Prophet; a blank page set before the divine pen. On this page there is no mark made by any other pen, no trace of profane or indirect knowledge. A prophet does not borrow knowledge from the human store, nor is he a man who learns in the slow human way and then transmits his learning. His knowledge derives from a direct intervention of the Divine in the human order, a *tajalli*, or pouring out of the truth upon a being providentially disposed to receive it and strong enough to transmit it. The purity of the stream of revelation remains unsullied in its course from the spring which is its origin to the lake into which it flows; in other words, the Qur'an exists in written form exactly as it issued from the divine Presence.[2]

It was out of this perfect submission that he became the complete *khalifa* of God. He was like a mirror turned to face all of God's Names and Attributes. The mirror itself does nothing, and (as it

---

2. Charles le Gai Eaton, *Islam and the Destiny of Man*, p 64.

were) *is* nothing. It is because of this submission, this *Islam*, that all the forms of life can appear within it. The Prophet was a shepherd, a businessman, a caravan-leader, a contemplative, a warrior, a diplomat, a legislator, a judge, a ruler, a man of his clan and his family, a father... but he was not thereby a 'Renaissance man', a person who seeks diversity of experience for its own sake, who develops and over-develops many and diverse talents because he is basically in flight from his true nature, and from the God who made him. He never departed from his Center in order to develop this or that side, or fragment, of his character. His character was unified, and beautiful, because it reflected the Unity of God.

As *khalifa*, Muhammad showed a perfect balance between mercy and wrath. He mirrored the truth of God's nature expressed in the *hadith qudsi*, 'My Mercy takes precedence over My Wrath.' Perhaps this does not sound like a perfect balance, since Mercy takes precedence, but the truth is that Mercy is the point of the Balance itself, while Wrath is that which overcomes imbalances and returns everything to Mercy. As Seyyed Hossein Nasr has said, 'the purpose of war is peace.' Likewise, the purpose of the inevitable imbalances brought us by life circumstances and our own psychology is to help us intuit our transcendent center of gravity, the point within us (yet beyond us) known as the Heart. In the words of the *hadith qudsi*, 'Heaven and earth cannot contain me, but the heart of my willing slave can contain Me.' The Heart is the light of God at the center of the human person. If the Heart is like the sun, the virtues may be compared to the rays of the sun, and to the many colors of the spectrum hidden in sunlight. The character of the Prophet Muhammad, peace and blessings be upon him, exhibits both the entire spectrum of the virtues and the perfect balance between them—the synthesis of all the Names of God known as the Muhammadan Light, whose receptacle, destined as such from all eternity, is the human form.

The root of polytheism is in the human psyche, which is why the greater *jihad* is called, not 'the struggle against the body' or 'against the world', but 'the struggle against the self'. The self we must struggle against is the *nafs al-ammara*, the 'commanding self'. This commanding self is the aspect of our soul which commands or incites us to evil. While we are at one with the commanding self, which is our condition before the struggle against the self has begun, we will not notice its commands because we are in the habit of obeying them automatically. But as soon as we start developing virtue and character, the *nafs al-ammara* appears as an enemy or inner saboteur which will do all in its power to prevent us from succeeding. While the struggle is going on, we are in the state known as the *nafs al-lawwama*, the 'accusing self'. Our conscience has begun to unfold, we have started to see our shortcomings, but we still don't have the power to overcome them. And when the greater *jihad* has finally been won, we come into the state known as the *nafs al-mutma'inna*, the 'self at peace', the soul perfectly submitted to God. According to some authorities, the self at peace is the same as the Heart; and certainly it is the way toward the Heart, toward the unity of character which will allow us to realize the Unity of Being (*tawhid*).

While we are under the power of the commanding self, however, we are true polytheists. Every fragment of the soul, every psychological 'complex' owns a piece of us. The gods and goddesses of polytheistic religions usually represent the main aspects of the human psyche: emotion, mental intelligence, self-love, sexual desire, aggression, hunger, the desire for possessions, etc. While these things are neutral and natural in themselves, they become good or evil depending on whether they are dedicated to God (and thus unified) or ruled by the commanding self (and thus at war with each other)— and until they are fully dedicated to God, which usually requires a long and serious struggle, they are commonly ruled by the commanding self.

As a child grows, he or she must develop the ability to feel purely, to think clearly, to have self-respect, to understand the meaning and requirements of his or her gender, to manifest appropriate strength, to eat in a healthy manner, and to use and maintain his or her possessions appropriately. As each one of these powers of the soul develops, the person is presented with the choice of either using it well or misusing it. It is at precisely these points of unfolding where psychological development becomes the struggle against the self. Weaning and toilet training, for a young child; learning good manners and how to defend himself for an older one; developing thinking skills for a still older one; and finally learning how to relate to the opposite sex and how to earn a living, are all parts of the greater *jihad*. It is true that, in terms of the religious life and the spiritual Path, the *jihad al-akbar* can take us far beyond these preliminary adjustments to the requirements of life, even to the point of (in the words of the Prophet, peace and blessings be upon him), 'dying before we are made to die.' But character must be developed before it can be sacrificed, though each step on the road of character-development is like a little death. We must die to passions, immaturity and childishness, and be resurrected in our full adult humanity.

The word 'character' in English originally meant a sign, a brand or a stamp. 'A man of that stamp' means a man of this or that particular character. The letters and image stamped on a coin give it its *character*. According to al-Ghazali in *Kitab Riyadat al-nafs*,

> A trait of character ... is a firmly established condition (*hay'a*) of the soul, from which actions proceed easily without any need of thinking or forethought.[3]

A thing's character is its essence, its true nature. Yet we talk about building human character, as if character were something that could develop over time. If our character is our true nature, isn't it something we were born with? Why do we have to develop it?

To say that someone 'has character' means that he or she has taken some real steps toward becoming a true human being. To have character means to be fully formed; to have no character, or a bad character, is to be undeveloped, or developed in an unbalanced way. Just as a body-builder who builds certain muscle groups but not others is not really well developed, someone who develops his mind but not his feelings, or his will but not his mind will be unbalanced. He will have flaws and weaknesses in his character.

So character is something we have to work on. But we need to develop it on the basis of who we really are as God made us. God

---

3. *Al-Ghazali, On Disciplining the Soul, Kitab Riyadat al-nafs and On Breaking the Two Desires, Kitab Kasr al-shahwatayn*, Bks XXII and XXIII of *The Revival of the Religious Sciences, Ihya 'ulum al-din, Abu Hamid al-Ghazali*, translated with introduction and notes by T. J. Winter (Cambridge: The Islamic Texts Society, 1995), p17.

'stamped' us with our true character before we were ever born; our job is to develop, to actualize, what God has stamped us with. Just as to 'envelop' means to wrap something up, to 'develop' means to unwrap something. Character development, then, is the process of *unpacking* what God has provided us for our journey through this world, and into the next. Various experiences during this life may *stamp* us and mold our character. But since all experiences ultimately come from God, everything we encounter in this life is part of God's knowledge of the character He has stamped us with, in eternity, before we came into this world.

In Arabic the word for character, with the connotation of good character, is *kluluq*, which is related to the word *khalq*, creation. Character is the form in which God has created us; our responsibility is to live up to it—to conform ourselves, in time, to the shape in which God has created us, in eternity. In Paradise, that shape will come to meet us *as* Paradise; in Hell it will stand over us, as an eternal reminder that we have failed to meet the mark of our own nature, and are therefore among the losers.

We develop character by practicing and realizing the *virtues*. The word 'virtue' is related to the word 'virility' (similar in meaning to *shahama*, manliness). We used to talk about the 'virtues' of herbs and stones—by which we meant their power to heal us, to make us complete. Virtue is power. It is the power to be who we really are, to attain and maintain the human state God has commanded us to embody. The virtues are what allow us to live up to the Trust God has placed upon us, which we as a race have willingly assumed (Q 33:72).They are what allow us to be *'abd*, God's slave, and *khalifa*, God's fully-empowered representative in this world—not only in our essential nature, by which we are *'abd* and *khalifa* from all eternity, but consciously and intentionally. Virtue is the power which allows our intent to match our nature.

According to the Qur'an 35:15, *O men! It is you who stand in need of God, whereas He alone is self sufficient. . . .* Only God is the Rich (*al-Ghani*) because Being itself can be attributed only to Him (*al-Qayyum*); we are so poor that we can't even claim Being for ourselves. If our very being is a gift from God, we certainly can't attribute any of the virtues to ourselves. All the virtues, all the powers, belong to God alone; they are His Names and Qualities. When we practice a virtue until we have fully embodied it, then our soul has been qualified with the Divine Name which corresponds to that virtue. We have been *stamped* by God with that Name.

The 99 Beautiful Names of God are the archetypes of all human virtues. This doesn't mean, however, that we can claim them in a simple way, which is why the names of the virtues don't strictly correspond to the Names of God. For example, God is the All-Powerful (*al-Qadir*). But He is not called 'the Courageous', because the human virtue of courage exists to overcome cowardice, and God cannot be cowardly. Nonetheless, all human virtue is still an irradiation of the Names of God upon the human form.

But if the virtues are gifts of God, why must we 'struggle in the way of God' to acquire and perfect them? This, of course, is one of the perennial questions of religion, the question of predestination and free will. Does God determine all our actions through His fore-knowledge? Or are we free to obey and disobey? The greatest minds have struggled with this question for many centuries, and have come up with a number of different answers. For example, the Mutazilites within Islam emphasized free will while the more ortho-dox Asharites tended to emphasize Divine pre-determination. But all we really need to know is that God, being the Omniscient, knows all things beforehand, that He *lets go astray whom He wills and guides aright whom He wills* (Q 74:31), and that we are still com-manded to do good and avoid evil. Qur'an is full of exhortations and warnings, on almost every page. If humanity had no free will, these exhortations and warnings would be meaningless.

It is impossible for us, as humans, to imagine what the mind of God is like; yet it may be permissible to say, following the words of friends of God to whom He has revealed some of his mysteries, that God both sees us in our eternal perfection, since He sees all things only as Himself according to His Name *al-Haqq*, the Truth, and also knows whether or not we are going to live up to that perfection, according to His Names *al-Alim*, the Omniscient, and *al-Muhsi*, the Knower of Each Separate Thing. But because God sees all things from the standpoint of His own eternity, according to His Name *al-Samad*, the Eternal, He doesn't *foresee* what we will do; it is as if, whether the act is in our past or our future, He sees us doing it right now—which is why He is named *al-Basir*, the All-seeing—and to watch someone doing something is not to make him do it. So his 'foreknowledge' doesn't destroy our freedom. As for guiding and leading astray whom He will, the Qur'an makes clear that He guides those who seek and submit to His guidance, and leads astray only those who are really asking for it: *it is He who lays the loathsome evil [of disbelief] on those who will not use their reason* (Q 10:100). So there is no question that we must struggle in the way of God to practice the virtues, as God has commanded. Nonetheless, every action we perform is, in essence, His action; He is *Al-Muqtadir*, the All-Determiner, and *Al-Jabbar*, The Compeller. His is the power by which we practice the virtues; His is the punishment we earn if we depart from them.

In order to practice the virtues more fully, however, we must know what they really are. The actions prescribed for us by the *shari'ah* are manifestations of the virtues; by practicing them, we gradually come to understand their less obvious implications; our character becomes more refined. But if to practice them helps us understand them, a better understanding of them also helps us practice them more effectively. Virtues are the actions we must perform in the greater *jihad*, the struggle against the commanding self; but they are also *truths*, penetrating insights, new ways of looking at things. To practice a virtue is to transform our experience of ourselves, society and our fellow human beings in very specific ways. To acquire a particular virtue is to train ourselves in how to see the signs of a specific Name of God in the world around us. On the level of human will, virtues are duties; on the level of the human intellect, virtues are knowledge; on the Divine level, as Names of God, virtues are spiritual realities.

There is no virtue, no Name of God which is not reflected in the character of the Prophet. All virtues are Muslim, just as all virtues are Hindu or Jewish or Christian or Buddhist. But since every revelation of God is unique, Islamic virtue carries its own particular 'fragrance', which is unmistakable. The following ten virtues, or constellations of virtues, are clearly visible in the character of Muhammad, peace and blessings be upon him. There is no virtue the Prophet of God did not manifest: we can't recount them all. But since ten is the number of perfection in Islamic tradition—reflected perhaps in the ten closest companions of the Prophet—we will concentrate upon these ten:

I

MERCY
(*RAHMAN*; *RAHIM*)

ACCORDING TO THE *hadith qudsi*, in which God Himself speaks through the mouth of the Prophet, 'My Mercy takes precedence over My wrath'. Wrath lives on the turbulent surface of the ocean of life; Mercy lives in the depths. Without Mercy, nothing would *be*; it is through Mercy alone that God creates the worlds. In the words of another *hadith qudsi*, 'I was a hidden treasure and wanted to be known, so I created the world that I might be known.' The power by which God creates the universe is known as *nafas al-Rahman*, The Breath of the Merciful.

And if the universe is a product of Mercy, what else could a God-given religion like Islam be, but an even more concentrated expression of the same Mercy? God doesn't need us; we need Him. If we transgress the *shari'ah* He has laid down, the loss is ours, not His; if we obey, the eternal gain is ours. Our very existence is a free gift of God's generosity, and the path He has laid out for us to return to Him is an additional Mercy: the word *shari'ah* literally means 'a path that leads to water.' Even the dire warnings that appear in the Qur'an are essentially nothing but the protective words of a Friend who doesn't want to see us lose our way and come to grief. And if our existence is a Mercy, and God's guidance a further Mercy, what better way to show gratitude for Our existence, and for God's sustenance and protection, than to extend Mercy to all creation?

The message which is to be conveyed in its integrity . . . by the Messenger has many facets, matched to the multi-faceted human personalities to whom it is addressed, but there is a golden thread which runs through the whole pattern of revelation and binds it together; this is the thread of mercy. Without the link provided by the second *Shahadah* and by the message—the Qur'an—to which it relates, this world would be like a frozen planet, too far from the sun to receive its life-giving warmth; this link is therefore itself an aspect of mercy. 'We sent thee not except as a mercy to the worlds' (Q 21:107). One of Muhammad's titles is the 'Key to Mercy', and mercy is the quality which presides over the road leading to God. 'A'isha asked him: 'Does one come to Paradise only by the mercy of Allah?' He repeated three times over: 'No one comes to Paradise except by the mercy of Allah!' 'Not even you, Messenger of Allah?' she asked. 'Not even I, unless Allah enfolds me in His mercy.'

He told his companions: 'When Allah completed the creation He wrote the following, which is with him above His Throne: 'My mercy takes precedence over My wrath', and this *hadith* is decisive for Muslims; it states categorically that all the 'names' and attributes by which the Qur'an indicates various aspects of the divine nature as they relate to humanity are subordinate to this supreme and essential attribute.

A desert Arab, seeing the Prophet kiss his grandson, said contemptuously: 'What, do you kiss children? We never do so!' to which the Prophet replied: 'I cannot help you, for Allah has withdrawn mercy from your heart.' Speaking in the first person in the Qur'an, God says: 'My mercy embraceth all things.' (Q 7:156), and this mercy communicates itself to those who are receptive: 'Indeed, those who believe and do good, the Merciful will endow them with loving kindness (*wuddan*)' (Q 19:96); and: 'Who else but those who have lost their way could despair of the mercy of their Lord?' (Q 15:56).[1]

A great part of Mercy is simply to restrain anger, whether or not it seems justified. This is called 'forbearance.' The Qur'an says,

But He will call you to account for what your hearts have earned, and Allah is Forgiving, Forbearing. (2:225)

And know that Allah is Forgiving, Forbearing. (2:235)

1. Charles Le Gai Eaton, *Islam and the Destiny of Man*, p 67.

And certainly Allah has pardoned them; surely Allah is Forgiving, Forbearing. (3:155)

And those who restrain their anger and pardon men; and Allah loves the virtuous. (3:134)

The Prophet said:

The most intelligent of people are those who are strictest in matters of courtesy and friendship; and the most prudent of them are those who most restrain their anger.

Whoever lives in courtesy and friendship dies the death of a martyr.

Allah never raises a man by his ignorance, nor abases a man because of his forbearance.

A believer will, by his forbearance and gentleness, attain the rank of a scholar who is struggling to solve problems of jurisprudence.

There are no two things which combine better than forbearance and knowledge.

When Allah revealed the verse, *Take to forgiveness, enjoin good and turn aside from the ignorant* [7:199], Gabriel said, 'O Muhammad, it means that you should be forbearing with the man who has insulted you, forgive the man who has wronged you and give to the man who has denied you something.'

PERHAPS the Prophet's greatest act of Mercy was his clemency to his former enemies, the Quraysh, after his conquest of Mecca:

Mounted on Qaswa, Muhammad rode into his birthplace unopposed and immediately proclaimed a general amnesty. 'This,' he said, 'is the Day of Mercy, the day upon which Allah hath exalted Quraysh.' He had come, not to destroy, but to rectify, and a noble people had been reborn. The historical consequences of this act of clemency were incalculable. Over the succeeding centuries no conquering Muslim general could enter a territory or city without knowing himself subject—on pain of damnation—to the obligation of mercy and the necessity to follow the example set that day; and this in turn led to countless conversions among people who learned forbearance from his example.[2]

The Qur'an says about forgiveness:

Take to forgiveness and enjoin good and turn aside from the ignorant. (7:199)

Repel [evil] with what is best, when lo! He between whom and you was enmity would be as if he were a warm friend. (41:34)

And if you pardon and forbear and forgive, then surely Allah is forgiving, merciful. (64:14)

When a man asked the Prophet to explain nobility of character to him, he replied: 'It means that you should forgive him who has wronged you, re-establish ties with him who has broken them off, give to him who has denied you something, and tell the truth even if it is against your own interests.'

According to Abu Bakr, the Messenger said: 'Be forgiving, for surely forgiveness only increases a slave in nobility; be forgiving to each other, and Allah will increase you in honour.' According to the same source, the Messenger said, 'Accept the excuse of anyone who justified himself, whether he be in the right or in the wrong; if anyone does not accept his excuse, then my intercession will not reach him.'

Al-Baqir relates that the Jewess who poisoned the sheep's flesh eaten by the Prophet was brought before the Prophet, who asked her, 'Why did you do what you did?' She replied, 'I told myself that if he is a prophet then it will not harm him, but if he is merely a tyrant, then the people will be free of him.' And according to al-Baqir, the Messenger forgave her.

The greater part of Mercy is simply good-hearted kindness. Of kindness, the Prophet said:

Kindness is prosperity and offensiveness is misfortune.

Never was kindness placed on something but that it beautified it, and never was it removed but that it marred it.

---

2. Charles Le Gai Eaton, *Islam and the Destiny of Man*, p127.

In kindness there is increase and blessing; whoever withholds kindness withholds goodness.

No two persons keep company with each other but that the one with the greatest reward and the most beloved of Allah is the one who is most kind to his companion.

If kindness were a visible creation, nothing which Allah has created would be more beautiful than it.

Kindness is especially due to those closest to us. No one who does not love his family will be able to love his neighbor—or God, for that matter. The Prophet, in his Farewell Address, directed Muslims to 'Take special care to be kind to your mothers and fathers, sisters and brothers, then those nearest of kin.'[3] The Qur'an says of kindness to parents:

And dutiful to his parents, he was not insolent, disobedient. (19:14)

And We enjoined man in respect of his parents. (31:14)

And that ye be kind to your parents. . . . Say not to them [so much as] 'Fie' nor chide them, but speak to them a generous word. (17:23)

And dutiful to my mother, and He has not made me insolent, unblessed. (19:32)

Al-Sadiq (Abu Bakr) tells of the time when a man came to the Prophet asking for permission to fight in the *jihad*, which was granted. The man said, 'O Messenger, I have two elderly parents who claim that they are so fond of me that they do not want me to leave.' The Messenger replied, 'Then stay with your parents, for by the One who has my soul in His hand, their fondness for you—be it only a day and a night—is better than fighting for a whole year.'

A man came to the Messenger asking for instruction. He replied, 'Do not associate partners with Allah in any way—even if you were burning in fire or being tortured—except if your heart was at peace in the certainty of faith; obey and be kind to parents, whether they

---

3. Zakaria Bashier, *Sunshine at Madinah* (Markfield: The Islamic Foundation, 1990), p130.

be alive or dead; and if they command you to leave your family and wealth, then do it, for this is true faith.'

A man asked the Messenger, 'What right does the father have over the son?' He replied, 'He should not call his father by name, nor walk nor sit in front of him, and he should not revile him.'

A man came to the Apostle, saying, 'O Messenger of Allah, whom should I treat kindly?' 'Your mother,' he replied. 'And then whom?' 'Your mother.' 'And then whom?' 'Your mother.' 'And then whom?' 'Your father.'

To extend Mercy is to allow God to adorn our souls with the qualities of His highest and most all-encompassing Name other than 'Allah' itself. Not for nothing does every *surah* of the Qur'an but one begin with the words, *In the name of God, the Merciful, the Compassionate.*

> *Forgiveness is the crown of noble qualities, [while] of all the acts of a powerful man, vengeance is the most odious.*

> —Hazrat 'Ali

II

SPIRITUAL POVERTY (*FAKR*)
DETACHMENT (*IHTISAB*)
HUMILITY (*TAWADHU*)

If you disobey worldly possessions,
worldly possessions will obey you.

—Hazrat 'Ali

ISLAM BEGINS WITH THE SENSE of the human being as *'abdu'Llah*,
the slave of God. The poverty of man in the face of the Absolute is
clearly evident in the life of the Prophet, beginning with his child-
hood experience:

> It was customary to send the sons of the Quraysh into the desert
> to be suckled by a wet-nurse and spend their early childhood
> with a Bedouin tribe. Apart from considerations of health, this
> represented a return to their roots, an opportunity to experience
> the freedom of the nomad and to learn, in a formative period of
> their lives, what it meant to be a Lord of Space, moving with the
> flocks and experiencing the impact of the changing seasons.
> Thus the bond with the desert was renewed in each generation,
> and the alliances formed in this way between Bedouin and
> townsmen were useful to both. A fatherless boy, however, was an
> unattractive investment. Muhammad was accepted by Halima,
> the wife of a shepherd of the Banu Sa'd, only because she was
> among the poorest of those who came that year to seek sucklings
> and could find no other. He spent four or five years with his
> Bedouin family, tending the sheep as soon as he was old enough

to walk, learning the ways of the desert and, according to traditional stories, bringing great good fortune to his foster parents.

When he was six, not long after he had rejoined his mother, she took him on a visit to Yathrib, where his father had died, and herself fell ill with one of the fevers prevalent in the oasis, dying on the return journey. The Arabs' fondness for children and the nature of the extended family assured the security of the orphan, and Muhammad now came under the guardianship of his grandfather, 'Abdu'l-Muttalib, chief of the Hashimite clan. The old man (he was in his eightieth year), although he had many children of his own—including a son, Hamzah, who was the same age as Muhammad—had developed a particular affection for his little grandson and made a point of keeping the boy with him when, as was his custom, he rested in the evenings on a carpet set down for him in the shadow of the Ka'ba. Here the two of them could watch the world go by, the one too old to participate and the other too young, while the great men of the Quraysh strolled past in the cool of the evening discussing the affairs of the city.[1]

His relationship to poverty, both inner and outer, continued in his later life; he was a living example of the Qur'anic verses, *O men, you are the ones who have need of God.* (Q 35:15), and *God was in no need of them. And God is All-sufficient.* (Q 64:6)

> Muhammad had no wish to live in any less Spartan fashion than did his people. His main meal was usually a boiled gruel called *sawiq*, with dates and milk, his only other meal of the day being dates and water; but he frequently went hungry and developed the practice of binding a flat stone against his belly to assuage his discomfort.[2]

The voluntary poverty of the Prophet flowed naturally from the realization that *All is perishing, except His Face* (Q 28:88) On one occasion he said: 'What have I to do with this world? I and this world are as a rider and a tree beneath which he shelters. Then he

---

1. Charles Le Gai Eaton, *Islam and the Destiny of Man*, pp100–101.
2. Ibid., p117.

goes on its way and leaves it behind him.' In the words of Hazrat
'Ali, 'Whoever attaches himself strongly to life makes himself a tar-
get for misfortune and the vicissitudes of fate.' Such *ahadith* are an
expression of the virtue of Detachment, *ihtisab*. Detachment has
nothing to do with holding yourself apart from people or avoiding
life, but rather with the ability to let come what God wants to send,
and to let go of what God wants to take away. As the Prophet's said,
'A man will not find sweetness of faith until he is heedless of the
fruits of this world.' He also said: 'Doing without (*zuhd*) in this
world does not mean wearing coarse clothes and eating coarse food,
but rather curbing one's expectations.'

Though not every Muslims is called to be an ascetic (*zahid*), a
certain degree of asceticism in are area of food is recommended for
all Muslims, since—according to al-Ghazali—overeating, along with
lust, is one of the two major barriers to the spiritual life. The Prophet,
peace and blessings be upon him, once said to A'isha: 'You should
beware of extravagance, and it is extravagant to eat twice in a single
day.' The modern world, however, has produced types of eating
disorders which al-Ghazali and the Prophet Muhammad probably
never heard of, such as *anorexia* (starving oneself in the deluded
belief that one is fat) and *bulimia* (overeating and then vomiting).
Such disorders, which affect women more than men, are signs of
what could be called *negative egotism*. Most traditional ascetics and
spiritual guides have tended to see egotism largely in its active
manifestations, like arrogance, gluttony, greed, lust and aggression,
and have recommended exercises to reduce this kind of excess. But
according to Al-Ghazali, egotism and vice appear not only as *excess*
but also as *deficiency*. And in our times we have seen how depression,
pathological self-hatred, self-mutilation and suicide, often among
young people, have become major social problems. These disorders
are signs of a character-*deficiency*, which is just as much a form of
egotism as the character-*excesses* of gluttony or arrogance or lust.
The commanding self may command us to worship ourselves; it may
also command us to damage and destroy ourselves. In both cases, it
has made sure that we are too involved in *thinking and worrying*
about ourselves, when we should be remembering God. Both excess
and deficiency in our character will interfere with our ability to sense

God's presence, which is just what the commanding self wants. Al-Ghazali therefore recommends moderation in eating, avoiding both the extremes of gluttony and self-starvation. He quotes Abu Sulayman as saying, 'If something is put before you in the nature of a desire which you have renounced, then partake of it just a little, but do not give your soul all that it hopes for. In this way you will banish a desire without making it pleasurable for your soul.' In the words of the Qur'an, *Eat and drink, but do not be extravagant.* (Q 7:31)

If asceticism were more socially acceptable in the secular societies, anorexia and bulimia might not be so common. It may be that such disorders are actually signs of an unconscious desire for spiritual purification which has somehow become distorted—most likely because secular society does not recognize spiritual purification as a real human need. In a culture which requires teenage girls to worship vanity and self-display, a deep spiritual desire to free themselves from the vanity culture—an unconscious attraction to Modesty and Spiritual Poverty—may lead girls to starve themselves. This, unfortunately, is a terribly ironic strategy, since the *conscious* desire of such anorexic girls is to avoid becoming fat and sloppy (as so many of their gluttonous friends actually are), so as to live up to the ideal of slimness the vanity culture sells them, even if they already look like walking skeletons. When they look into the mirror they see themselves as fat; but the truth is they are fat with self-involvement, not weight. Unlike those desperate teenagers, usually boys, who violently act out, sometimes murdering teachers and classmates, the anger of these girls against the spiritual starvation in their lives is turned against themselves. The following story has to do with the relationship between gluttony and starvation, as well as that between starvation and anger:

> Once upon a time there was a moody and violent king who kept a pack of huge, vicious dogs in a cage in the palace dungeon. The dogs were underfed and always hungry. Anyone who displeased the king was immediately thrown to these monsters and devoured.

> A wise friend of God became a courtier to this king. The king showered him with favors, yet he was not at ease. The king's

mood-swings were notorious, and the wise man had already seen too many of his fellow courtiers thrown to the dogs. So he made it a habit of visiting these dogs. When he approached their cage they barked and snarled, but he always had a large piece of raw meat with him, which he threw between the bars. Finally the dogs learned to jump up and wag their tails whenever he approached.

Then one day what the courtier feared finally happened: some trivial event involving him threw the king into a rage, and he ordered him thrown to the dogs, as he had done so many times with others in the past. The guards were summoned, and the wise man dragged off to the dungeon.

Soon, however, the king began to feel remorse. This was his favorite courtier, his boon companion. How could he have been so cruel and impulsive? So he called his guards again and had them run to see after the unfortunate courtier, the king himself following on their heels. But when they arrived in the dungeon, what should they see but the courtier surrounded by his friends the dogs, fawning on him and licking his hands.

'A miracle!' the king cried. 'I should have known that my dogs would have no power over a man of God; only forgive me for my heedlessness and violence.'

'This "miracle" has a simple explanation, O king,' the courtier replied, and he proceeded to tell him how he had escaped death. Upon hearing the truth, the king was mortified. He reinstated the courtier as his favorite, and had the dogs destroyed. From that day forward he was known as a moderate and just ruler, his moodiness and violence cured.

Hot, impulsive anger (as opposed to cold, calculating hatred) is based on a rebellious desire for things to be different than they are, *right now*—which is why the man or woman who is perfectly submitted to the will of God's is no longer dominated by anger. And there is no better way to approach this submission than to 'fast' from time to time from our desires and obsessions—to just say 'no' to them. Whether our obsession is to eat too much or to starve ourselves, whether it is to arrogantly assert ourselves or to damage and destroy ourselves, the act of deliberately denying the commanding self what it wants—not necessarily all of the time, but certainly some of the time—is the straightest path to Spiritual Poverty. To say 'no' to the *nafs al-ammara* is the best way to break one's identification with it, and learn in a very concrete way how the *nafs* is something distinct from, and often opposed to, the spiritual Heart.

One of the virtues most closely related to Poverty is Humility (*Tawadhu'*). *And the servants of the Beneficent are they who walk on the earth in humility, and when the ignorant address them, they say: Peace.* (Q 25:63) According to the *hadith*, 'My Lord gave me the choice of being one of two things: either to be a slave and a messenger, or a king and a prophet, and I did not know of which of the two to choose. At my side was the angel Gabriel, and when I raised my head he said, "Be humble to your Lord," so I replied, "A slave and a messenger."'

Humility is based on a clear sense that, in the presence of God, we are as nothing—and that we are never not in the presence of God: to realize one's nothingness in the face of God is the root of Islam. We may work to develop such humility because we recognize that it is praiseworthy, or that it is one of the virtues of the Prophet that we wish to imitate, but only the sense of God's real presence can bring this virtue to perfection. And even if we don't feel the keen sense of God's presence, we can still act as if we did. In the Prophet's words, 'pray to God as if you saw Him, because even if you don't see Him, He sees you.' Furthermore, if you know that you are in the presence of God right now, you will realize that, as far as you are concerned, all things, persons and situations are signs of God which have something to say *to you*, while you yourself are far from perfect in your ability to pay attention *to them*.

Al-Ghazali names *fawning* and *ostentatious self-abasement* as among the vices; neither has anything to do with real humility. To make submission *to another person's ego* is not truly humble, since it is almost always done for some kind of personal advantage, besides being a form of idolatry in itself. The respect we owe to our superiors is part of the respect we owe to God; we do not fulfill our duty to Him by turning those superiors into little gods. And humility should never be ostentatious; it ought to be obvious that to make a big show of one's humility is not a very humble thing to do.

In the words of the Prophet, peace and blessings be upon him, 'The most troubled people are the kings, the most hated the proud, and the most abased those who treat others with contempt.' He also said: 'When the slave humbles himself then Allah raises him to the seventh heaven.'

All Muslims have a chance to deepen their understanding of the perishable nature of creation, and the eternity of God's face, during the fast of Ramadan; nothing humbles us, and shows us our essential nothingness, like physical weakness. If even a change in our eating schedule can confront us with our inherent poverty, how poor we must be—except as we are rich in Him.

III

COURTESY (*ADAB*)
MODESTY (*HAYA'*)
DISCRETION
(*HUSN AL-TADBIR*)

Everything must be in accord with reason,
and reason itself must be courteous.

—Hazrat 'Ali

ONE OF THE CENTRAL MUSLIM VIRTUES, so apparent in the character of the Prophet, is Courtesy (*adab*). The Prophet said, 'Gabriel kept on recommending [that I treat] the neighbors in a kind and polite manner, so much so that I thought that he would order me to make them my heirs.'

According to 'Abdullah bin 'Amr, 'The Prophet never used bad language. . . .' He also used to say 'The best amongst you are those who have the best manners and character.'

Courtesy is based on a recognition that the dignity of the human state is not limited to oneself, nor to those who are great or fascinating or powerful in worldly terms. Every human being is an expression of the human essence, the *fitrah*; therefore every human being is, potentially, *khalifa*, God's fully-empowered representative in this world, whether or not he or she is faithful to this Trust.

We can never know for sure whether a particular person is living up to their responsibility as *khalifa*, or betraying it. When, after the Prophet took Mecca, his former sworn enemies, like Abu Sufyan and Hind, embraced Islam, no one could be blamed for wondering about their sincerity. Yet to openly question that sincerity would have been the height of discourtesy. We can never know the secret of the relation between another human soul and its Creator; this is the origin of the Muslim blessing 'may God keep his secret.' In the words of the Prophet, peace and blessings be upon him: 'Do not look for the faults of the believers. Whoever seeks after the faults of his brother, then Allah will seek after his faults; and whoever Allah looks for in search of his faults then He will discover, even if he is hidden in his house.'

No human being wants his greatest and most intimate delights, or his most shameful and secret sins, spied upon by a stranger. And in a religion where one's relationship to the community of fellow believers is central, it is even more important for Discretion (*Husn al-Tadbir*) to be observed in our relations with others. When one's person is seen daily in the mosque and the market place, it is all the more essential that one's heart, and the hearts of others, be treated as *haram*—a word which refers to something which is forbidden because it is sacred. A person's secret relationship with God is *haram*—and the 'stranger' who is most likely to pry into and disturb this relationship is one's own egotism and vanity.

Courtesy in Islam has many aspects, and perhaps the largest part of it is to maintain good relations with one's own family, and fulfill one's duties to them. *And we have enjoined in man respect of his parents* (Q 31:14); *And that ye be kind to your parents. . . . Say not to them [so much as] 'Fie' nor chide them, but speak to them a generous word* (Q 17:23). Among the duties one owes to one's children is to give them a good education, starting in infancy: The Prophet said, 'Whoever has a new-born child should say the call to prayer in his right ear and the call to start the prayer in his left—this is a protection against the accursed Satan.' Equally important is Courtesy and affection between husbands and wives. *And treat them [the wives] kindly* (Q 4:19).

The Prophet said, 'The believer with the most perfect faith is he who is most courteous and kind with his family'; he also said, 'The best of you are those who treat their wives best, and I am the best of you in the way I treat my wives.' As for sexual relations, the Prophet advised, 'No one should mount his wife like an animal: let their be communication between them'. When asked what that communication was, he replied, 'Kissing and talking.' Marriage is a covenant between two parties, both of whom have their rights: *And they have made with you a firm covenant* (Q 4:21). In the words of the Prophet, peace and blessings be upon him, 'Maintaining good family relations increases one's numbers and wealth, gives life to one's people, and is a staff for the weak at the time of death.'

Courtesy, of course, must also to be extended to one's neighbor: According to Al-Bara' bin 'Azib, 'Allah's Apostle ordered us to do seven things . . . : to follow the funeral procession, to visit the sick, to accept invitations, to help the oppressed, to fulfill the oaths, to return the greeting and to reply to the sneezer: (saying, 'May Allah be merciful on you,' provided the sneezer says, 'All the praises are for Allah').' Among the most important points in Muslim courtesy according to the prophetic *ahadith* are greeting people with *asalaamu alaikum*; shaking hands and kissing; sitting and standing in a correct and courteous manner; asking permission before entering another person's house; giving gifts; adopting other Muslims as brothers; respect for the elderly; respecting your neighbor's rights; visiting each other, especially the sick; befriending the poor; and accompanying the corpse to the grave. According to the *hadith qudsi*, 'Those who love each other for My sake are worthy of My love, and those who visit each other for My sake are also worthy of my love.'

The Qur'an enjoins:

And when those who believe in Our commandments come to you, say: Peace be on you (6:54)

Do not enter houses other than your own houses until you have asked permission and saluted their inhabitants. (24:27)

The believers are but brethren, therefore make peace between your brethren. (3:103)

The Prophet said:

If one of you meets a brother, then he should greet and shake hands with him, for Allah has bestowed this on the angels—so do as the angels do.

When a man is content to sit without distinction and honors in company, Allah and his angels bless him until he rises.

It is a mark of respect for a fellow Muslim when you accept a gift from him that you present him with something of your own and do not obligate him with anything.

Treat the elderly with deference, for deference to the elderly is honoring Allah, and whoever does not treat them with deference is not one of us.

Whoever causes harm to his neighbor, God will deprive of the breeze of the Garden.... Whoever does not fulfill the rights of his neighbor is not one of us.

If a slave visits his brother for the sake of Allah, a voice calls from Heaven, 'Prosperous are you and prosperous are your steps; a house has been built for you in the Garden.'

Visit graves and thereby remember the next world; wash the dead, for doing this is rewarded and it is a profound lesson; pray over the dead that it may make you grieve, for the one who grieves is under the protection of Allah.

Visit your sick and comfort them with prayer, for surely this is equal to the prayer of the angels.

Whoever assists the poor and is just with people of his own accord is a true believer.

Courtesy is intimately related to *Modesty* or *Shame* (*haya'*). It is narrated on the authority of Abu Huraira that the Prophet (may peace be upon him) said, 'Iman has over seventy branches, and modesty is a branch of Iman.' He also said, 'There are two kinds of modesty: the modesty of the intellect and the modesty of foolishness. The modesty of the intellect is knowledge; the modesty of foolishness is ignorance.'

In a sense Modesty is Courtesy in relation to oneself; it is a part of self-respect. Only if we respect ourselves will we be able to respect others; there is nothing more discourteous to other people than violating our self-respect by acting immodestly or shamefully. It is narrated on the authority of 'Imran b. Husain that the Prophet (may peace and blessings be upon him) said: 'Modesty brings forth nothing but goodness.'

Discretion is the part of Courtesy which prevents us from stripping someone else of their Modesty. The importance of Discretion in Islam can be measured by the degree of seriousness attributed to the vices of slander and gossip and backbiting; this is why it is said that the heart of a true friend is 'the grave of confidences'. To repeat something told to you in confidence is an act of betrayal, comparable to stealing something from a person's house and selling it on the open market—except in this case you are stealing something from a person's soul. To reveal secrets about another person, and to desire to hear them revealed, is to claim a right which is God's alone. How Godlike and omniscient we sometimes feel when gossiping; it's as if we were recreating in our own image the person we are gossiping about. But only God can create a human being; all the human mind can create is a caricature of a human being; and if we turn other people into caricatures, we are in danger of becoming caricatures ourselves. Al-Baqir said:

> [Among] the most beloved of my companions ... are those who best refrain from telling others of our conversation; the worst and most hated of them for me are those who, if they hear the conversation, ascribe it to us and narrate it as coming from us.

Through the virtue of Modesty we protect ourselves against being gazed upon by strange eyes—and by the prying eyes of our own commanding self, which must be prevented from spying upon our secret relationship with God, and perverting it. If we know for certain that God sees all we do and all we are, we will not be tempted ask others to validate us by displaying our virtues, nor will we tempt others to judge us by displaying our sins. Only God can validate us; only God can judge. The Prophet said: 'Pray to God as if you saw Him, because even if you don't see Him, He sees you.' This is the root of Courtesy. If we are not just intellectually but also *emotionally* certain that we are always in the presence of God, if we understand that He has first claim on our intimacy, then we will not demand *absolute* intimacy from others, which is something that no-one can really give. We will no longer try to command other people's attention; we will stop prying into their affairs. In the words of the

German poet Ranier Maria Rilke, 'love . . . consists in this, that two solitudes protect and border and salute each other.'

Courtesy has to do with *respect*, which means 'to look again.' Our 'first look' at someone is the casual glance. If, after making eye contact, we continue to gaze at someone casually, as if we were watching a movie or looking at an inanimate object, we have violated Courtesy. Our 'second look' must be one of respect; it must include the recognition that the other person is now looking too, and knows that we are looking. And even if the other is not looking, we must remember that God is. To gaze on someone without their knowledge is to violate their unique relationship with their Creator, which is *haram*.

To ogle and peep at other people, whether or not this is sexually motivated, is to treat them as objects. It is to say, in effect, 'I am the one who is real, the one who is conscious; this other one only exists through my consciousness of him; he is not a person in his own right; he is nothing but a part of *my* experience.' When a given society loses its belief in God, or at least its concrete sense that God is actually watching, people turn each other into objects in just this way. We forget that we are dependent for our very existence upon God's attention to us; we treat our separate individuality, our ego, as if it were God. And when we no longer experience ourselves as dependent upon God, we become dependent upon each other for our very *feeling of existence*. We include the other within the circle of our ego as if he or she were a personal possession, and then demand that the other do the same with us. All this is a violation of Modesty. In the Prophet's words, 'Allah has mercy on the slave who feels true modesty in the face of his Lord, who protects his mind and what it perceives.'

In popular psychology, this kind of immodesty is called *codependency*. Codependency is based on a lack of respect and Courtesy, and ultimately a lack of objectivity: without some sense of God as the absolute Reality, we are at the mercy of our own subjectivity because we have no point outside that subjectivity to turn to for a 'reality check'. If we have forgotten our total dependency upon God, then there is nothing left for us but to try to depend upon other people's attention to us, because without such attention we don't even feel like human beings. Instead of paying attention to God, we become beggars for the attention of others, constantly trying to make them pity us or look up to us. But this is not true human relatedness, only mutual idolatry.

It goes without saying that we must depend on each other in many ways. We need emotional support and human love, and society cannot function well to maintain human life unless every member contributes. But the true Sustainer, the true Beloved, is always God. Everything else, the institutions of society, the ways in which human beings support and bless and exhort and protect each other, is really nothing but the play of His Names in the field of this world.

So our first intimacy is with God. But this intimacy is not to be taken for granted. If we must avoid taking each other for granted, how much more must we avoid taking God for granted! God knows and sees all things; He knows us better than we know ourselves. But His intimacy with us does not guarantee ours with Him. He may be *nearer . . . than the jugular vein* (Q 50:16), while we, through forgetfulness and inattention, are still very far from Him. So Courtesy and Respect and Modesty are as necessary in our relationship with God as in our relations with our brothers and sisters—even more so, in fact. In the words of the Prophet, peace and blessings upon him, 'Be as modest before Allah as you would before one of your people who is spiritually advanced.'

The Prophet attained perhaps his greatest intimacy with God during his Ascension, his *miraj*. The Qur'an (53:16–18, Pickthall translation) says of this event: *When that which shroudeth did enshroud the lote tree, the eye turned not aside nor yet was overbold.* The *lote tree* perhaps represents the limit of what can be known about God. When this overpowering vision of God was hidden, the Prophet's attention *turned not aside nor yet was overbold*; he was neither indifferent nor curious; he neither became distracted, nor did he pry into the Divine Mysteries. Here we see the root of courtesy in the human relationship to God. When you are before the Throne of the King, it is impolite to boldly stare, and equally impolite to let your attention wander—or to sulk, or to fawn, or to make demands. You must simply wait, in humility, in vigilance, in self-respect, upon the King's good pleasure.

This is the basic *adab* to be followed in the act of remembering or contemplating God. And the same *adab* applies in human relation-ships. It is impolite to ignore someone, unless they have let you know that this is their wish. It is also impolite to force your atten-tion upon them, or to try to hook and control their attention. To maintain the balance between curiosity and indifference, so that you and the other person can begin to mutually define the correct border between you, according to the unique shape of the present moment, is what Courtesy is all about.

Courtesy, however, does not always seem modest. It is not simply a passive virtue. Sometimes strong intervention is needed to re-establish Courtesy in a situation where it has degenerated or been betrayed. The following story is told of one such intervention:

Among the people of Medina there was a particularly ugly little man called Zahir.

The Prophet was fond of him, and seeing him one day in the mar-ket, came up behind him and slipped his arms around his waist. Turning in surprise, Zahir shouted 'Who's this?' and then, seeing who it was, leaned back against the Prophet's chest. The Prophet called out: 'Who will buy this slave from me?' 'Alas,' said Zahir, 'you will find me worthless goods, I swear by Allah.' 'But in the sight of Allah you are by no means worthless,' said the Prophet.[1]

It takes a master of Courtesy to know when the apparent viola-tion of Modesty actually serves Courtesy in a higher sense. But in a society without a general regard for Modesty, no such act of chiv-alry as the Prophet exhibits here is possible. You can't know when it's appropriate to cross the line of formal etiquette if you can't even see the line.

Abbas Husain gives this description of the Prophet's character and *adab*:

He was shy and would not stare into people's faces. He answered the invitation of the slave and the free-born and he accepted pre-sents even if they consisted of merely a drop of milk or a rabbit's leg. He ... visited the sick, attended funerals of his enemies

---

1. Charles Le Gai Eaton, *Islam and the Destiny of Man*, p 121, n 2

without a guard. He was the humblest of men. Silent, without being insolent. Most eloquent, without being lengthy. He was always joyful and never awed by the affairs of this world. He rode a horse, a male camel, an ass. He walked bare-footed and bare-headed at different times. He loved perfumes and disliked foul smells. He sat and ate with the poor. He tyrannized nobody and accepted the plea of those who begged his pardon. He joked, but only spoke the truth. He laughed but did not burst out laughing. . . . He was always the first one in greeting. In a hand-shake, he was never the first to release his hand. He preferred his guest to himself and would offer the cushion on which he reclined until it was accepted. He called his companions by their *kuniyat* [names of paternity or maternity] so as to show honour to them. Children, so as to soften their hearts. One did not argue in his presence. He only spoke the truth. He was the most smiling and laughing of men, in terms of his companions, admiring what they said. He never found fault with his food. . . . If he disliked it, he did not make it hateful to someone else. . . . Hazrat 'Ali, his closest companion, said: Of all men, he was the most generous, most open hearted, most truthful, the most fulfilling of promise, the gentlest of temper and the noblest to his family. Whoever saw him unexpectedly, and who ever was his intimate, loved him. He himself said: 'I am the complete, perfect man.' . . . The ultimate miracle of the Prophet lies in the perfect courtesy on a day to day basis . . .*consistency* is it.

Calling the Prophet's consistent courtesy 'the ultimate miracle' may seem like only a figure of speech, an exaggerated way of expressing admiration for a person universally admired. But in another way it is the simple truth. A true story is told of a dervish who was visiting other dervishes belonging to a different group. These dervishes were known for indulging in *karamat* or miraculous feats. One of these feats was to cut themselves with knives and swords while under the influence of a spiritual state (*hal*), without drawing blood or leaving any wound. While the visiting dervish looked on, one of the dervishes of this group drew a razor-sharp sword, then leaned against it until it cut deeply into his belly. The visiting dervish, not being used to miraculous occurrences, jumped up and ran over to his brother dervish, anxiously asking him if he was injured, if he needed help. 'Fool!' Said the miracle-worker. 'Of course I am not injured! Have you no experiences of such things in your order? I need fear nothing, the power of Allah has protected me.' And so it was; when he withdrew the sword, no blood appeared, neither was there any wound.

What can we learn from this story as it relates to *adab*? Perhaps the lesson is that although the miracle-worker had enough spiritual power to cut his belly with a sword and remain uninjured, he did not have enough to avoid injuring his brother through discourtesy and arrogance, demonstrating that the power required to be courteous is greater than the power required to perform miracles.

A BIG PART of Modesty and Courtesy, or the lack of them, is expressed in the way we dress. It's not simply that we should be modestly covered; it is equally important that our dress should be appropriate to the dignity of the human state—which is why cross-dressing, for example, is strictly forbidden in Islam.

The Muslim should dress neither like a *fop* nor like a *slob*. As for foppery, the Prophet forbade men to dress in silk: 'Allah's Apostle ... forbade ... to wear ... silk [clothes], Dibaj [pure silk cloth], Qissi and Istabraq [two kinds of silk cloths].' As for dressing like a slob, the generally dignified dress of the traditional Arab offered a degree of protection against this extreme—which is not to say that there aren't some western styles of dress which are relatively elegant without being ostentatious. Among the modern-day problems the Prophet never had to face, however, were the habit of deliberately dressing in an ugly manner—called the 'grunge' style in the United States—and of wearing clothes with corporate logos and printed advertisements. To dress like this is extremely discourteous, both to yourself and to those who have to look at you, even if neither you nor they are aware of it. Courtesy, like all virtues, is an objective reality; just because someone doesn't recognize that he is in fact being insulted, or is himself insulting others, does not make the insult any less destructive. In the modern world we insult ourselves every day, in innumerable ways, without even realizing it; the effect is simply to lower our self-esteem and make us touchy and quick to take offense.

To deliberately dress in ugly or torn clothes is to let everyone know that you have no self-respect, and are ashamed at nothing. And to dress as a walking advertisement is to advertise that you worship *Nike* or *Adidas* in the place of Allah. To dress as if you had self-respect will help teach you self-respect; to dress as if you had no shame you will lead you toward shameful acts, and attract the attention of people who are without shame themselves.

If 'heaven and earth cannot contain Me, but the heart of my believing slave can contain Me' *(hadith qudsi)*, then we all possess a precious secret which must not be disclosed to others except at the time and place God determines. In the symbolism of the two sexes—which is close to the mystery of God's relationship to His Creation, expressed in Qur'anic verses such as *And of everything We created a pair* (51:49)—it is the woman who more directly represents this secret; this is the basis of the institution of *hijab*, the woman's veil—which, of course, is open to many different interpretations. According to Zarakia Bashier, for example, [*Sunshine at Madinah*, p170], 'hijab . . . was never meant to act as a curfew upon the movement of Muslim women. Nor was it meant to work against their having a public role in Muslim society.'

However feminine Modesty is outwardly expressed in different places and times, the inner Modesty which protects God's secret relationship to the human soul is always absolutely commanded. If a women's inner modesty is deep enough, it will protect her spiritual secret more powerfully than any veil; it is the veil which serves the secret, not the other way around. The value of the veil in tempering male lust is only a special case of the value of spiritual Modesty in tempering our desire to pry into the secrets of God. As the Prophet said, 'Faith is naked, and its clothes are modesty.' In the case of men, the most common way Modesty is violated is through *looking*; for women, it is most commonly violated through *revealing*. Yet women, too, can sin through looking; this is called curiosity. And men can certainly sin through revealing; this is called vanity and ostentation.

The sweetness of life lies in dispensing with formalities.

—Hazrat 'Ali

IV

GENEROSITY (SAKHA')
HOSPITALITY (NUZUL)

THE PROPHET WAS AN OCEAN OF GENEROSITY; he was generous
not only with his goods, but also with his labor, his teaching and his
presence:

> It was only too well known that 'he could refuse nothing.' One
> day a woman gave him a cloak—something he badly needed—
> but the same evening someone asked him for it, to make a
> shroud, and he promptly gave it up. He was brought food by
> those who had a small surplus, but he never seemed to keep it
> long enough to taste it. There was always someone in greater
> need.[1]

After his conquest of Mecca, the Prophet was not only merciful to
the defeated Quraysh, but generous:

> To complete the reconciliation Quraysh were treated with the
> utmost generosity over the following months; Abu Sufyan,
> instead of losing his head, received a gift of two hundred camels.
> Understandably, the *ansar* began to feel resentful. 'O Helpers!'
> the Prophet said to them; 'Are you stirred in your souls concern-
> ing the things of this world by which I have reconciled men's
> hearts, that they may submit to Allah, while you I have entrusted
> to your *islam*? Are you not well content, O Helpers, that these
> people take with them their sheep and their camels, while you
> take with you the Messenger of Allah in your homes?' They were

---

1. Charles Le Gai Eaton, *Islam and the Destiny of Man*, p 117.

content; but already one senses a division—which would grow more pronounced as time went by—between the people of this world and the people of Paradise.[2]

The Prophet said of Generosity:

The Garden is the abode of the Generous.

Generosity is one of the trees of the Garden which reaches down to the earth; whoever takes a branch from it will be led to the Garden by that branch.

Gabriel has related that Allah has said, 'As for Myself, I am content with this religion—only generosity and good character are fitting for it, so ennoble it with these two as far as you are able.'

Provision comes more quickly to the one who feeds others than the knife to the hump of a camel; and Allah boasts to the angels about the one who feeds others.

The generous man is close to Allah, close to the people, close to the Garden and far from the Fire.

The Prophet was also great in Hospitality. The virtue of Hospitality is important in Islam not only because survival in the desert, where Islam began, is impossible without it, but because every person's household, as a place of intimacy hidden from the eyes of the world, carries the quality of something that is forbidden because it is sacred. The admission of someone to this *haram* space is, consequently, a most precious gift. The same sentiment is to be found in two English proverbs: 'A man's home is his castle', and 'home is where the heart is'. In an important sense the traditional Muslim house, built of strong, usually windowless outer walls surrounding an inner courtyard and garden open to the sky, is a true symbol of the Heart. And the deepest and most sacred hospitality is that through which the truths of the Heart are shared. Hospitality involves giving, not just of one's goods, but of oneself.

A central aspect of Generosity and Hospitality is to give with an 'open hand', which entails not looking down upon those in need. To

2. Ibid., pp127–128.

give 'with strings attached', in order to create a sense of shame or obligation in the recipient, is not generosity but commerce; this is why secret charity will always have its place. As Hazrat 'Ali said, 'Hide the good you do, and make known the good done to you.' In a society like that of early Islam where the vigorous contribution of each Muslim man or woman was necessary for the survival of the community, it would have been all too easy to look down upon the needy as 'parasites', especially when the need was based on a 'tender-minded' character which requires stillness and time for reflection as much as food or water or air. But this was not the Prophet's way:

> Enterprise was encouraged, but there were also those of a more contemplative temperament who had neither the skills nor the inclination to earn their own living, and they—as though to prove that the Muslim does not have to be an 'activist'—were given an honoured place in the community. A space was found for them to sleep in the covered section of the new mosque and they came to be known as 'the People of the Bench'. They were fed with food from the Prophet's own table, when there was any to spare, and with roasted barley from the community chest; and of all these the most famous was Abu Huraira, which means 'Father of the little cat', who followed Muhammad everywhere—just as his little cat followed him—and to whose prodigious powers of memory we owe a great number of recorded *hadiths*. Perhaps he might be regarded as the first of those of whom Muhammad was to say: 'The ink of the scholars is more valuable than the blood of the martyrs.'[3]

If the giver is truly generous, he will not violate the self-respect of the one in need. And for the needy one to receive a gift with true gratitude, neither fawningly nor arrogantly, is also an act of generosity, since it prevents the giver from feeling unappreciated or degraded. Furthermore, the same *adab* applies when it comes to accepting gifts from God. He is *Al-Karim*, The Generous; His Generosity is free and unmerited—but woe to us if we take it for granted! Among His greatest gifts to us is the opportunity to be

3. Ibid., pp 116–117.

grateful to Him—and, in His Name, to those who extend His Generosity and Mercy to us in a way that our hands can touch and our eyes can see.

Gratitude (*shukr*) is one of the greatest blessings the soul can receive, and one of the easiest and most natural forms of inner purification. It is a manifestation of God in His Name *Al-Shakur*, The Grateful. The grateful soul is naturally humble without either resistance or self-abasement. Gratitude is of the essence of Generosity, since it is a treasure which cannot be kept, but must be given. But we must not expect nor depend upon gratitude in the recipient of our gift. It is better for us if we so completely forget the gift we give—since to give something means to let go of it, and this means releasing it from the grasp of the mind and the emotions as well as the hand—that we take no notice of any ingratitude on the part of the recipient, and are sincerely puzzled by his gratitude.

According to Ibn Ata'illah, the descent of good fortune divides humanity into three groups: those who attribute everything to fate, or their own cunning; those who recognize all as coming from God alone, with no regard for His agents; and those to whom God grants the power to extend gratitude to His agents as well—the actual human beings through whom His generosity has appeared—without forgetting that, in reality, all gifts are from Him; gratitude to those who are generous to us is actually gratitude to the Generous Himself. Ibn Ata'illah names the third of these groups as the most mature and complete.

> *These two belong to generosity:*
> *To give of one's possessions,*
> *and to protect one's honor.*
>
> —Hazrat 'Ali

V

TRUSTWORTHINESS (*AMANAH*) VERACITY (*SIDQ*) SINCERITY (*IKHLAS*)

WHEN THE HOLY QUR'AN descended upon Muhammad, peace and blessings be upon him, on the Night of Power, its effects were shattering. He confessed to Khadijah that he feared he had become a poet or a psychic—an unbalanced person subject to psychic or spiritual 'states' without enough character-strength to withstand them. But this was not the case. Abbas Husain comments:

> When we understand something from the depth of our being, we sometimes lose control. We burst out. We're happy for days. We are in a daze. We know of poets, who having come up with something really wonderful are then unable to continue ... this joy that bubbles up. The sight that you get into the nature of reality. Consider all this and consider this is the person on whom the Qur'an came line by line. This is the person on whom it kept coming for twenty-three years, ten months and five days. So crushing was this experience that he said that he would burst out in a cold sweat even if it were winter. If he were sitting on a camel, the camel would sit down. Consider the pulverizing nature of the divine revelation. And now consider that he never had a gap in his day to day activities.

This is Trustworthiness incarnate—and the guardians of Trustworthiness are Veracity and Sincerity. According to Javad Nurbakhsh, Veracity (*sidq*) is 'being truthful with God and the creation, both outwardly and inwardly, and being what one shows oneself to be,'[1] while Sincerity *(ikhlas)* 'is that, without paying attention to any creature or taking into account the gratification of your own self, you think, do and act for God.'[2] So Veracity relates more to being, Sincerity more to action. Whoever possesses the virtues of Veracity and Sincerity will be trustworthy in his dealings with others, keeping his or her promises and fulfilling his or her responsibilities. In Shakespeare's words, 'to thine own self be true/And it must follow, as the night the day/Thou canst not then be false to any man.' To be true to yourself is not to follow the passions of your commanding *nafs*, but to be faithful to your *fitrah*. To be true to yourself is to see yourself objectively, to be honest about your own strengths and weaknesses. If you are objective with yourself, you have taken a big step toward realizing the Prophet's *hadith*, 'die before you are made to die.'

Whoever is objective about himself will also be able to see the things, persons and situations around him objectively, since he will no longer be 'projecting'. *Projection*, a term taken from psychoanalysis, means falsely seeing something in another person, or in circumstances, that is really in you. If you know yourself, you will not project; you will see yourself and other people truly and clearly, in line with the prayer of the Prophet, 'O Lord, show me things as they really are.' God in His Name *Al-Haqq* is Absolute Truth—which is why the objective truth in any situation, the truth that is really there whether or not we are aware of it, is a real aspect of His Presence. This is one meaning of the *hadith*, 'He who knows himself knows his Lord.'

If you are true to yourself, you will gain the power to speak the truth. Firstly, you will be able to speak the truth because you will *know* the truth, which includes knowing both what you *do* know and what you *do not* know. Veracity entails admitting the limits to your knowledge and not filling in the space of your ignorance with

---

1. Javad Nurbakhsh, *Sufism V* (London and New York: Khaniqahi-Nimatullahi Publications, 1991), p91.

2. Javad Nurbakhsh, *Sufism IV* (London and New York: Khaniqahi-Nimatullahi Publications, 1988), p105.

fantasies and suppositions. Secondly, you will be strong enough to speak the truth because you are used to facing up to things honestly, both in circumstances and in yourself, including things that are not necessarily in line with your hopes or expectations. And you will also gain the power *not* to speak the truth when silence is more appropriate; you will develop the virtue of Discretion (*husn al-tad-bir*). To speak the truth is not always to serve the truth.

The most common title of the Prophet Muhammad, peace and blessings upon him, is *al-Amin*, 'the Trustworthy,' based first of all on his reputation as a merchant and caravan-leader. The following story illustrates this virtue in the Prophet's character:

> In the year 605 the governing council of the Quraysh, the *mala*, decided that the Ka'ba should be rebuilt. Although this temple of Abraham is, in essence, timeless, its earthly form—being perishable—has been reconstructed a number of times. In that year a Byzantine ship had been wrecked on the coast, providing excellent timber for the purpose, and there was a Christian carpenter living in Mecca who was competent to erect the scaffolding. The main work of construction was divided between the clans, but when it was done, disagreement arose as to who should have the honour of replacing the sacred Black Stone in its niche. It was decided that the first man to enter the square by a particular gate should be asked to act as arbitrator, and the first comer was Muhammad. He told the people to bring a large cloak, placed the stone on it and called upon representatives of each of the clans to join together in raising it into position; he himself then fixed the stone in its niche.[3]

This story beautifully illustrates how Trustworthiness and Objectivity are aspects of the same virtue. The competing claims of the different clans are like the endless conflicts that arise between different opinions, conflicts which tempt those involved to care more about *being right* than about discovering *what is true*. They are also like the many different and competing voices we often hear inside us when we are faced with a hard decision. When the Quraysh

3. Charles Le Gai Eaton, *Islam and the Destiny of Man*, p102.

submitted their dispute to the unexpected, they submitted it to God's will. When they accepted Muhammad as arbiter (according to the Name of God *al-Hakam*, The Abritrator), they submitted to God's decision. And when Muhammad came up with a plan which allowed every clan to have a part in replacing the Black Stone,[4] he was manifesting a sign of God's Objectivity, which transcends the many and various desires and opinions of you and me. He was also demonstrating how God's Objectivity is also His Unity: only that which is beyond us (God in His Name *al-Jami*, The Uniter) can truly unite us.

The Qur'an says of Trustworthiness: *If one of you trusts another, then he who is trustworthy should deliver his trust.* (2:283) And the Prophet, peace and blessings upon him, said of Trustworthiness and Veracity: 'Do not look to how much they pray, fast and go on the *Hajj*, their kindly actions and their murmuring of prayers in the night, but rather look to their telling the truth and guarding what is entrusted to them.'

Consider not who speaks, but what is said.

—Hazrat 'Ali

4. The Black Stone symbolizes a number of things: Spiritual poverty (*fakr*); the blackness of the unknowable Divine Essence (*al-Dhat*) which appears black to us only because its light is too intense and dazzling for us to see; and also our *fitrah*, our original 'adamic' human nature. In Adam's time, according to legend, the stone was white, but over the aeons it became blackened by the sins of humanity. When the alchemists speak of producing 'the philosopher's stone,' they are talking about a return to our original essence as God made us, about becoming 'people of substance,' simple, weighty and rock-solid. It is this essence which makes us worthy of acting as *khalifa*, of assuming the Trust. (Q 33:72).

VI

FEAR OF GOD
(*KHAWF*)

Except for the fear of God,
I would be the most cunning of the Arabs.

—Hazrat 'Ali

To FEAR GOD means to both to fear His future punishment for our transgressions, and to stand in awe of Him in the present moment. In the first case, Fear of God protects us from performing evil actions; in the second, it prevents us both from doing evil and from letting our attention wander when we should be attending to Him.

Of the Fear of God, the Qur'an says:

And for him who fears to stand before his Lord are two Gardens. (55:46)

And for him who fears to stand in the presence of his Lord and forbids the soul from low desires, then surely the Garden—that is the abode. (79:40–41)

They fear their Lord above them and do what they are commanded. (16:50)

But do not fear them . . . fear Me, if you are believers. (3:175)

Then whoever fears My guidance, no fear shall come upon them, nor shall they grieve. (2:38)

Those who fear God's future punishment—who encounter Him in His names *Al-Darr*, The Punisher, and *Al-Muntaqim*, The Avenger—are being called by Him to repent; and so Fear is an aspect of Mercy, since God is also *Al-Ra'uf*, the All-Pitying, *Al-Ghaffar*, He

Who is Full of Forgiveness, and *Al-Ghafur*, the All-Forgiving. Yet those who fear for the future, whether their fear be of material suffering or spiritual punishment, are still veiled from God. Such fear is certainly a spiritual opportunity, but it is not yet a complete virtue, and may in fact be a vice: a lack of Trust in God.

The Fear of God manifested by the Prophet Muhammad, peace and blessings be upon him, was not a fear for the future, but rather an awe and terror in the face of God's Majesty in this present moment. According to Ansari,

> Daqqaq says: 'Awe is a precondition of knowledge of God. As God says, "God warns you to beware of Him" (Q 3:28).' (*Resala-ye qoshayriya*). The fear of the elect resides in their awe of Majesty, not in their fear of chastisement. Fear of chastisement is to worry for oneself and one's welfare, but awe of Majesty is reverence for God and forgetfulness of self.[1]

The revelation of the Holy Qur'an came upon the Prophet in an awesome manner, like the rumble of distant thunder:

> A need for solitude possessed him and drove him out of the busy city into the rocky hills and wastelands which surround Mecca. There he was seized by certain premonitions and visions, sometimes frightening and sometimes 'like the coming of dawn.' Little is known concerning the exact nature of these experiences, but the accounts that have come down to us suggest that a great force—a light, a splendor—was approaching ever closer, and, like a bird beating with its wings against a window-pane, trying to reach him through the membrane which isolates us in our little world of experience. Such an approach must have its repercussions in nature, which trembles before the power of unseen dimensions. We are told that the world of stones and rocks and barren valleys seemed to Muhammad to have come to life; he heard strange voices calling, and he covered himself in his cloak, fearing death or madness in the embrace of some dark power. It seemed as though the demons which cluster in such desert places

---

1. Javad Nurbakhsh, *Sufism II* (London and New York: Khaniqahi-Nimatullahi Publications, 1982), p 3.

and buzz about the traveler's ears pursued him even to the cave in which he took refuge on Mt. Hira.

His family and friends observed the change in him with increasing anxiety, but there was nothing he could explain to them; there was no way in which he could have understood that his deepest nature was being, as it were, forged anew—its receptivity laid bare—during these solitary vigils, full of terror and expectation. In the blaze of day and during the clear desert nights, when the stars seem sharp enough to penetrate the retina of the eye, his very substance was becoming saturated with the 'signs' in the heavens, so that he might serve as an entirely adequate instrument for a revelation already inherent in these 'signs'. It would come when he had been made entirely ready. . . .

[On *Laylat 'l-Qadr*, The Night of Power] Muhammad was asleep in the cave on Mt. Hira. He was awakened by the Angel of Revelation, the same who had come to Mary the mother of Jesus, Gabriel (called by the Arabs Jibra'il), who was clothed in light and who seized him in a close embrace. A single word of command burst upon him' *Iqra*'—'Recite!' He said: 'I am not a reciter!' but the command was repeated. 'What am I to recite?' he asked He was grasped with an overwhelming force and thrown down, and the first 'recitation' of the Qur'an came upon him: 'Recite in the name of thy Lord who created—created man from a clot. Recite, for thy Lord is Most Bountiful, who teacheth by the pen, teacheth man what which he knew not. . . .' (Q 96:1–5)

Muhammad was forty years old and he had grown to maturity in the world. The impact of this tremendous encounter may be said to have melted his substance. The person he had been was like a skin scorched by light and burnt away, the man who had come down from the mountain and sought refuge between Khadija's breasts was not the same man who had climbed it.

For the moment, however, he was like a man pursued. As he descended the slope he heard a great voice crying; 'Muhammad, thou art the Messenger of Allah and I am Jibra'il.' He looked upwards, and the angel filled the horizon. Whichever way he turned his head, the figure was still there, inescapably present. He hastened home and called to Khadija: 'Cover me! Cover me!'

She laid him down, placing a cloak over him, and as soon as he had recovered himself a little, he told her what had happened.

She held him against her body, giving him, as it were, the earthly contact which saves a man's sanity after such an encounter. She reassured him with human reassurance and believed in the truth of his vision. When she had settled him and he had fallen into a deep sleep, she want at once to see her cousin Waraqa, one of the *hunafa* (these were isolated individuals who rejected idolatry, seeking the knowledge of the One God either in the tradition of Abraham or through Christianity.)

After listening to her account of her husband's experience, Waraqa told her, 'By Him in whose hand is the soul of Waraqa, if what you say is true there has come to Muhammad the great *Namus,* even he who came to Moses. Truly Muhammad is the prophet of this people. Calm your husband's fears and banish your own!'[2]

In addition to the terror of a direct confrontation with the Majesty of God, there is another fear of God, resulting from Awe, which is related to Vigilance (*muraqaba*) and Wariness (*taqwa*). This fear is based on the realization that no one can be righteous on his own without God's grace, that a misstep on the spiritual path is always possible, and that if we do not follow the norms God has laid down for us and continually implore His guidance, He Himself will lead us astray. This fear is like the fear of someone walking up a dangerous mountain path in the dead of night, with no light apart from Trust in God, and no way of insuring his safety except by taking great care where he places his steps. Night does not last forever, but while it does, Fear coupled with Trust is our only protector, just as panic—Fear without Trust—is among our greatest enemies.

The Prophet once said: 'When a man fears God, God makes all things fear him; but when he does not fear God, God makes him fear all things.' And in the words of Hazrat 'Ali, 'If you are able, increase your fear of Allah while at the same time having a good opinion of Him; the best of actions is to achieve a balance between fear and hope.'

2. Charles Le Gai Eaton, *Islam and the Destiny of Man*, pp102–103, 104.

VII

TRUST IN GOD (*TAWAKKUL*)
PATIENCE (*SABR*)
CONTENTMENT (QANA'A)

THOSE WHO FEAR GOD IN THE RIGHT WAY will develop Trust in Him. Their Fear will place them in the correct relationship to Him; it will make them pious, vigilant, and obedient. And since God is The Just (*Al-'Adl*), The Ever-Relenting (*Al-Tawwab*) and The Loving-Kind (*Al-Wadud*), those who keep to the Straight Path need not fear God's punishment. They will retain their sense of Awe, but it will be an Awe that develops into Trust—something like the feeling of being lifted up and carried in the palm of a vast and mighty Hand, a Hand that is steady as bedrock, and at the same time swift as a flying cloud. Trust in God is not the naive belief that what we fear will never happen and that what we hope for will come to pass. It is the knowledge that, since the worlds are created and destroyed only through Mercy, whatever God does with us is best for us—better than we could possibly imagine. This is the virtue of Contentment.

After the Prophet reached certainty with regard to the manifestation of the Holy Qur'an, after he knew that it was really God Who was speaking to him, that he was God's chosen Prophet, his Trust in God was perfect. (It was virtually perfect even before this, otherwise God would not have chosen him.) And though God will not likely send the angel Gabriel to speak to us and support us in our struggles, we as Muslims inherit from the Prophet, in a certain sense, his own Trust in God—at least virtually. He is the Seal of the Prophets, and we are sealed with that seal. Certainly we must realize this Trust as an active virtue in our own lives, but we need not ask for a revelation from God before we decide to trust in Him. We already have all the proof we need; the Holy Qur'an is the proof.

In the days after the Qur'an was revealed to Muhammad, peace and blessings be upon him, Fear gradually gave way to Trust:

> Some further revelations came to Muhammad—it is not known precisely which or how many—and then the heavens were silent for some weeks, perhaps for many months. Darkness descended upon his spirit. However terrifying the great vision might have been, the angel's absence was even more disturbing, for he was now left alone with his human weakness. It was as though a crack had opened in the carapace which encloses this world, so that he had seen and heard things which make the ordinary life of mankind appear unbearably narrow and suffocating; now it had closed. Having been taken out of the world and made a stranger to his own people, he found himself abandoned in a kind of no man's land between heaven and earth. He had asked Khadija, 'Who will believe me?' and she had answered, 'I believe you!' But this was love speaking. How could he expect others to believe when he himself was in doubt as to the nature of his vision?
>
> The fear of insanity, which had been with him for some time, now became acute. He had seen such people often enough: lunatics raving about the 'unseen', aliens in the community and objects of scorn to the sensible, heard-headed townsmen. He himself had always been a practical man, a man of business, and he belonged to a race which tends to take a down-to-earth view of things and to regard spiritual extravagance with suspicion (a dreamer would not survive for long in the desert.) Walking alone in the hills, hoping for some relief, he came to a sheer precipice and his foot dislodged a stone, which tumbled into the abyss. He was seized by the impulse to follow it. 'I wanted,' he said long afterwards, 'to find lasting repose and to rid my soul of its pain.' It is said that he was about to throw himself over the cliff when the angel's voice intervened, saying: 'Muhammad, you are the true Prophet of Allah!' He returned home, and soon after this a fresh revelation came to him: the *Surah* called *ad-Duha*, 'The Morning Hours'.

By the morning hours and by the night when it is most still, thy Lord hath not forsaken thee nor doth he hate thee. Truly that which is to come shall be better for thee than that which came before, and truly thy Lord shall give unto thee and thou shalt be well pleased. Did He not find thee an orphan and shelter thee? Did He not find thee wandering and direct thee? Did He not find thee needy and enrich thee? Therefore oppress not the orphan, neither repulse the beggar, but declare the goodness of thy Lord.[1]

It is easy to believe we have Trust in God when we feel the power of His presence. But just as God created the night to follow the day and the day the night, so he also created the day and night of the Spirit. Sometimes we feel His presence, sometimes His absence. He makes Himself present to us in order to manifest His Mercy, and absent from us so that we will not mistake *our experience* of His presence for His ultimate Reality. His presence gives us Hope (*raja'*) and Trust; His absence breaks our attachment to His gifts, and reminds us that our love and submission must be for Him alone. Every virtue is perfected in just this way, through our experience of the relentless alternation between God's strength and our weakness; to endure this alternation requires, and teaches, the virtue of Patience (*sabr*). Our weakness is the place where His strength is perfected; our nothingness is the throne where His Reality is established. And when we come to the station where we experience both His absence and His presence equally as signs of His Reality, then Patience has ripened into Trust, and Trust into Contentment. (In reality, God's presence never departs or diminishes; it is our own receptivity to Him which is fickle, which comes and goes; but God is constant.)

Of Patience, the Qur'an says:

Seek assistance through patience and prayer; surely Allah is with the patient. (2:153)

And if you are patient and guard against evil, truly that is an affair of great resolve. (3:186)

---

1. Charles Le Gai Eaton, *Islam and the Destiny of Man*, p 105.

Surely I have rewarded them this day because they were patient, and they indeed are the triumphant. (23:111)

In the words of the Prophet:

There are four kinds of patience: patience in longing, in anxiety, in doing without, and in expectation. Whoever longs for the Garden no longer thinks of desires, whoever is anxious about the Fire turns away from what is prohibited, whoever does without in this considers trials and tribulations easy, and whoever expects death hastens to perform good deeds.

And the Prophet said of Contentment:

The world is a series of changes in fortune: such benefit as you may draw from it comes to you despite your frailty, and what is to your disadvantage will afflict you without your being able to ward it off. Anyone who ceases to long for what has passed him by finds peace of mind, and whoever is content with what Allah has provided for him will find coolness for his eyes.

He also said: 'Contentment is an inexhaustible treasure,' and 'Whoever desires to be the richest of people should be more certain of what is in the hands of Allah than in the hands of men.'

VIII

COURAGE (SHUJAʿA)
MANLINESS (SHAHAMA)

OF COURAGE AND COWARDICE, the Prophet had this to say:

The nobility of the believer is in his wariness [in the face of temptation]. His aristocracy is in his religion. His manliness is in his good character. Boldness and cowardice are nothing but instincts which Allah places wherever He will. The coward shrinks from defending even his father and mother, and the bold one fights for the sake of combat itself, not for the sake of spoils. Being slain is but one way of meeting death, and the martyr is the one who offers himself, expecting his reward from Allah.

The instinctive boldness the Prophet speaks of here is not the same as the virtue of Courage or Manliness. We're not simply born with Courage; we must work to develop it.

The virtue of Courage grows, in part, out of the virtue of *Khawf;* when the Fear of God occupies the heart, it leaves no room for any other fear. There is the Courage to see, the Courage to feel, the Courage to question, the Courage to take an unpopular stand, the Courage to ask for help, the Courage to bear one's burdens in silence, the Courage to act, and the Courage to refrain from acting. Courage is the virtue—along with Vigilance—which gives us the ability to practice every other virtue. What is Generosity, or Trustworthiness, or Patience, or Dignity, without Courage? The central nature of the virtue of Courage is denoted by the English word for it, which means 'the quality of having heart.' In the words of the Qur'an, *Establish worship and enjoin kindness and forbid iniquity, and persevere whatever may befall thee. Lo! That is of the steadfast*

heart of things. (31:17) The Prophet Muhammad, peace and blessings upon him, possessed both the Courage to act and the Courage
to endure (*ihtimal*). During his ten years in Madinah he organized
seventy-four military campaigns, leading twenty-four of them in
person—though Abbas Husain has estimated that during his entire
life he spent no more than 89 days in battle. But his Endurance, and
his Suppression of Rage (*khazm al-ghayz*) were also great. This was
evident during the period of oppression the Muslims endured in
Makkah before the *hijra*, especially in the year when both his
beloved wife Khadijah and his protector Abu Talib died:

> . . . . the neighbors of the Prophet who were opposed to him,
> under the leadership of Abu Lahab and his wife, intensified their
> campaign of persecution. The Prophet used to remove the
> unclean refuse which they repeatedly threw inside his yard and
> in front of his door, complaining in a markedly restrained voice:

> 'What kind of neighborhood is this, O Sons of Abu Manaf?' But
> the worst incident of persecution which the Prophet experienced
> after the death of Abu Talib is narrated by Ibn Ishaq as follows:

> 'Then Khadijah bin Khuwaylid and Abu Talib died in the same
> year. Misfortunes continued to befall the Messenger of Allah,
> salla Allahu 'alayhyi wa sallam, as they could not hope to inflict
> upon him during Abu Talib's life. One of their insolent mob even
> heaped dust and earth upon his gracious head. As he entered his
> home, one of his daughters wept passionately as she wiped the
> dust from her father's head.

> 'Do not cry, my daughter,' he said, 'for Allah shall protect your
> father.'[1]

In order to develop Courage, we need to be honest with ourselves
about what we are really afraid of. There is physical Courage, moral
Courage and spiritual Courage. Physical Courage is the Courage to
risk our physical well-being. Moral Courage is the Courage to risk
psychological discomfort or social obloquy in order to do what is

---

1. Zakaria Bashier, *Makkan Crucible* (Markfield, Liecester, UK: The Islamic
Foundation, 1991), p180.

right; it may require us to face the uncomfortable fact that we are not who we thought we were, or that people we believed we knew are radically different from our mental image of them. And spiritual Courage is the willingness to acknowledge, in the face of Absolute Reality, that we ourselves are nothing—the willingness to be annihilated in the presence of God.

Spiritual Courage—whether virtual or fully actualized—is the root of moral and physical Courage. It is possible to have a degree of moral Courage in service to principles and ideals, and to take personal satisfaction in it, but such Courage is imperfect because in this case our real 'lord' is our own self-image, not the principles we claim to serve. True Courage in service to principles will make us willing to sacrifice in their name not only our physical well-being but also our moral self-satisfaction.

As for physical Courage, there is a kind of raw bravery which delights in danger. Such bravery is one element of true Courage, and can sometimes ripen until it reaches the level of that virtue. But physical bravery can also be a form of sensationalism and self-indulgence; a way of avoiding the call to develop moral and spiritual Courage; even an unconscious impulse to suicide, which Islam expressly forbids. (Bukhari relates on the authority of Abu Huraira that the Prophet said: 'He who commits suicide by throttling shall keep on throttling himself in Hell Fire (forever), and he who commits suicide by stabbing shall keep on stabbing himself in Hell Fire (forever).') It can also lead to physical cruelty, since those who are cruel to themselves may feel no compunction about being cruel to others. According to Al-Ghazali, one the virtues directly related to Courage is *khazm al-ghayz*, Suppression of Rage. In the words of Hazrat 'Ali, 'Anger is a raging fire. Whoever can subdue his anger puts out the fire; whoever cannot gets burnt himself.' Anger so often deludes us; it convinces us that it is power. But my own anger, the anger of the *nafs al-ammara*, is only weakness. God's anger alone can truly be called power.

Sometimes a person with a great deal of physical bravery will dream of dying a hero—in other words, of sacrificing his body on the altar of his ego. He would rather 'live' as a memory in the mind of his people than as a human being placed upon this earth by God to serve Him, and to be eternally united with Him after death. An attraction to physical danger requires, and helps us develop, a strong physical vigilance and awareness, but we may also indulge in it as an excuse for not developing subtler kinds of vigilance and awareness on the moral and spiritual levels. And if our real aim is self-destruction, even physical vigilance may be compromised. The true martyr is not the one who throws his life away, but the one who places that life in service of a moral ideal which is itself subordinate to the one spiritual Reality, even if this means certain death. Not every Muslim, of course, is required to die in the lesser *jihad*, but all are called to die in the greater one. In the words of the Prophet Muhammad, peace and blessings be upon him, 'die before you are made to die'. There are some whose death in the greater *jihad* will only become perfect at the moment when they come face to face with death in the lesser one; nonetheless, while the life of nature requires physical death of both the hero and the coward, with no necessary reference to religion, the religious life specifically requires the death of the ego. This is the true aim and ultimate purpose of Courage.

> *Courage and truth are always found
> together—like falsehood and cowardice.*
> —Hazrat 'Ali

IX

JUSTICE (*'ADL, QIST*)

No one can forgive who has not the power to punish.
—Hazrat 'Ali

JUSTICE IS ESSENTIALLY BALANCE; to do Justice is to correct imbalances, in outer situations as well as within your own soul. The central criterion of Justice in Islam is the Holy Qur'an, which at times contradicted the personal opinions and criticized the behavior even of the Prophet himself. Once when he was giving audience, a blind man tried to get his attention in a way that annoyed him; he frowned and turned away. In response to this, he received the *surah* 'He Frowned', which corrected his behavior. The blind man could not see the Prophet's frown, but the people could—and so could God. The Qur'an is teaching us here that no-one, not even His chosen Prophet, is perfect in essence; only God is perfect. But we are also being taught, through the Prophet's example, that it is possible to perfectly accept God's reproof; in this perfect *islam* we can see the true sublimity of the Prophet's station.

The Qur'an has the following to say about the human virtue of Justice, and about the Justice of God:

Maintaining His creation in justice, There is no God save Him [Allah], the Almighty, the Wise. (3:18)

O ye who believe! Be ye staunch in justice, witnessing for Allah, even though it be against yourselves. (4:135)

Lo! Allah enjoineth justice and kindness. (16:90)

And if two parties of believers fall to fighting, then make peace between them. And if one party of them doeth wrong to the other, fight ye that which doeth wrong till it return unto the ordinance of Allah; then, if it return, make peace between them justly, and act equitably. Lo! Allah loveth the equitable. (69:9)

[When] the earth shineth with the light of her Lord, and the Book is set up, and the Prophets and witnesses are brought, and it is judged between them with truth, and they are not wronged. (39:69)

The Prophet said, 'If Allah and his Apostle did not act justly, who would act justly?' The following are some exemplary stories of Justice from the life of Muhammad, peace and blessings be upon him:

[Consider the case of the Prophet's wife] Sawdah bint Zam'ah, who migrated twice to Abyssinia, and whose husband was one of the pioneering Muslims who, after his return from Abyssinia, died in Makkah. Marrying her was a way of honouring her sacrifice, and the early Hijrah to Abyssinia. It was also a way of consoling and providing for her.[1]

In the case of the Jewish tribe of the Bani Qurayzah, who broke the *sahifa*, the constitution of the first Muslim state which they had pledged to uphold, who betrayed the Prophet, the Muslims and the other Jewish tribes of Madinah at the Battle of the Ditch by secretly conspiring with the attacking Quraysh, Justice showed its most rigorous face:

Nothing is worse, in Arab eyes, than betrayal of trust and the breaking of a solemn pledge. It was time now to deal with the Bani Qurayzah, and they were told to choose an arbiter who would decide their punishment. They chose the head of the clan with which they had long been in alliance, Sa'd ibn Mu'adh of Aws who was dying of wounds received at Uhud and had to be propped up to give judgement. Without hesitation, he condemned the men of the tribe to death, and the sentence was carried out.

---

1. Zarakia Bashier, *Sunshine at Madinah*, p144.

It is doubtful whether any incident in the Prophet's life shocks the Westerner more deeply than this....Ours is a century in which in which there has been greater slaughter than in all the preceding centuries put together, and we find it acceptable to kill any number of people, including women and children, provided this is done at a distance and never on a one-on-one basis. Yet these same slaughterers of the innocent shrink from executing a traitor who is undermining the very structure of their society, or a criminal whose crimes are so hideous that his continued existence is an offense to humanity.[2]

I would add that in this instance, according to how wars were waged in the Prophet's time, and indeed in any place or time where society is organized on a tribal basis, every capable male member of the tribe is defined, in one way or another, as a combatant, whether or not he is on the front lines. There are no male 'civilians', much less conscientious objectors; there is no way to 'opt out'. And to betray one's companions-in-arms to the enemy in wartime is a capital offence in the armies of most modern Western democracies, not simply in the armies of societies which we would class today as archaic or theocratic.

An essential aspect of Islamic Justice is balance and strict limitation in war-making. Women and children are not to be deliberately attacked; noncombatants are not to be harmed. (Buhkari relates, on the authority of 'Abdullah bin 'Umar: 'Allah's Messenger disapproved the killing of women and children.') And no one is to be attacked because of his or her religion:

The effort to fight against religious oppression was called *Daf 'Allah* (the repelling for God) ... war is sanctioned ... so long as it ... is directed against those who resist by force the Islamic effort (*Da'wah*) to establish Allah's authority on earth.... If unbelievers do not attempt by use of force to obstruct the Muslim's effort to establish Allah's authority on earth, then the Muslims would have no justification for waging war against them, according to the verses of *Surah al-Hajj*. Their mere refusal to

2. Charles Le Gai Eaton, *Islam and the Destiny of Man*, p124.

accept Islam would not be a valid justification for war against them. Otherwise, the Muslims themselves would become repressors of religious freedom, and an oppressive power fighting people because of their convictions or religious belief.[3]

When the Prophet Muhammad (God plunge him in glory!) was drawing near death, he availed himself of one last chance to practice Justice:

> He came to the mosque wrapped in a blanket and there were those who saw signs of death in his face. 'If there is anyone among you,' he said, 'whom I have caused to be flogged unjustly, here is my back. Strike in your turn. If I have damaged the reputation of any among you, may he do likewise to mine. To any I have injured, here is my purse. . . . It is better to blush in this world than in the hereafter.' A man claimed a debt of three dinars and was paid.[4]

Since Islam is not only a religion but also a social framework—or rather a divine revelation in which, by virtue of the *shari'ah*, religion and society (ideally at least) are one—the question of *social justice* is central to the tradition. And the most important question when it comes to social justice is *the correct relationship between rights and duties.*

In Islam, man's essential 'right' is to choose God or reject Him; according to the Qur'an, *There is no compulsion in religion.* (2:256) It is true that human actions are divided into five categories: praiseworthy, permitted, indifferent, discouraged and prohibited. And certainly acts which are praiseworthy, permitted or indifferent could be defined as those we have a 'right' to perform. But human conduct in Islam is defined more in terms of duties than of rights. Clearly we have a *right* not to be oppressed—but since Islam is a religion, our moral duty before God and our neighbor must always come first, which is why our right not to be oppressed is most accurately defined in terms of our *duty not to oppress.*

3. Zakaria Bashier, *Sunshine at Madinah*, p 90.
4. Charles LeGai Eaton, *Islam and the Destiny of Man*, p 129.

Justice, in Islam, is fundamentally related not to self-assertion, but to Mercy. This is certainly not to say that the oppressed are not enjoined to seek and establish Mercy and Justice, if necessary by militant means. But this *jihad* to establish a just and merciful society is not to be carried out according to the paradigm of *rebellion*, where the *desires* of the dispossessed are asserted over against the *desires* of the privileged. The paradigm of *jihad* is not the rebellious assertion of desire, but faithfulness to one's human duty to God, by which personal desire in the realm of the soul is dethroned, and God established a the sovereign ruler of that realm; and so the greater *jihad*, the struggle against the self, is the source and archetype of the lesser. Desire is the 'pretender,' but God is the true King. Since God is Just, His rule also allows room for the moderate and dignified fulfillment of desire—but this is first an expression of His Mercy, and only secondarily of our rights. Insofar as humanity stands, as *'abd*, before the Absolute Truth, Power and Mercy of God, the concept of 'rights' disappears—except for the one truly inalienable right, the 'right to be what we are', the right—which is equally a duty—to embody the *fitrah*, to be who God made us to be, and commands us to be. Whatever social forces stand in the way of our fulfillment of this command do indeed violate our human rights.

But humanity is not only *'abd*; we are also *khalifa*. And as such, we certainly do possess 'inalienable rights'. The root of human rights, from the Islamic perspective, lies in the 'theomorphic' nature of man: we have the right, as well as the duty, to stand as representatives of God's Mercy and Justice in this world. And inseparable from this right is the right not to have our Dignity as *khalifa* violated. We do have the right—which is also a duty—not to submit to degradation at the hands of others, because whoever degrades a human being degrades God's image on earth. It is possible to suffer oppression with Dignity, as the Prophet did in the early years of his ministry in Makkah; but the time may come when submission to oppression becomes complicity in the degradation of that Dignity, at which point it is one's *duty* to assert one's rights.

Yet the assertion of our rights must never take the form of rebellion against God—as it did, for example, in the French Revolution. God may subject us to material and psychological hardship, but He never violates our essential human Dignity, since He Himself is the principle of that Dignity. And if we really believe this, then we possess the secret which will give us the power to deal with any hardship, any degradation that life throws our way. If we see hardship as coming to us by way of other people's arrogant and selfish actions alone, we will feel degraded; if we see it as coming by way of impersonal circumstances alone, we will feel oppressed. But if we know it ultimately as coming from no one but God, then we will recognize it as a test, or as purification, or as Justice; our human Dignity will in no way be compromised by hardship and suffering. The society founded by the Prophet in Madinah was based on a social contract which included both duties and rights; no society which does not define the rights of its citizens can ever be just. Nonetheless, any truly Islamic social system must be based first and foremost on man's duty to God; human rights can only be defined, and pursued, in light of this duty. As *khalifa* we can and should assert our rights; as *'abd*, we must recognize every right as a gift of God, and be careful not to 'bite the hand that feeds us'.

As followers of the religion of Islam, we do not demand from God the fulfillment of our needs and desires; we obey His commands, and trust in His Mercy. Islam thus includes an aristocratic element to complement its democracy; God is our Lord, and we are His servants, His vassals. The Irish poet William Butler Yeats defined the democratic character as one which struggles against circumstances, and the aristocratic character as one which first and foremost struggles against itself. The democratic element is charitable and sentimental, the aristocratic one honorable and passionate. In Islamic terms, the lesser *jihad* would thus be democratic and the greater *jihad* aristocratic. Aristocracy, like democracy, is made up of rights as well as duties, and both democratic and aristocratic elements are clearly visible in the Arabic character, and the character of the Prophet, upon whose example the Muslim character as a whole is based. In relation to others, the Muslim is a democrat precisely because he recognizes the inherent 'aristocracy' of the human soul.

THE HIGHEST LEVEL OF JUSTICE requires that we do Justice without demanding it, recognizing that our own demands—on our friends, our family, our neighbors, our employer, or our government—may themselves be the major imbalance in our immediate situation, and the only one we really have the power to put right. A story is told of Dhu l'Nun, the great Egyptian saint. There was a drought in Egypt, and the people implored him to pray to God for rain. He did so, and during his prayer God informed him that he himself was the source of the drought. So he left Egypt, and the rain came.

In the words of Hazrat 'Ali, 'the best form of justice is succoring the oppressed'—not only the politically oppressed, but also those who are made outcasts, ignored or ridiculed by society. Injustice is basically imbalance—and one of the great imbalances in worldly society is *imbalance of attention*. Those who are powerful or charismatic command all the attention, while those who are not, no matter how sincere or virtuous they may be, are deprived of it. Attention is like food: to crave it is a form of gluttony, but to be severely deprived of it is a kind of starvation. And while it is the better part of virtue not to *demand* attention, the virtue of Justice requires that we *give* everyone the attention he or she needs—no more, but certainly no less. In the *hadith* literature we see how the *sunnah* of the Prophet was to make no distinction between the great and the humble in granting audiences (though in the course of things he naturally spent more time with his close companions than with anyone else). This openness to approach became the model and the ideal for all future Muslim rulers.

One of the Names of God is *Al-Adl*, 'The Just'. Some people have a hard time understanding how God can be just, since the world is filled with injustice, and nothing happens that is not God's will. Jalallu'd-din Rumi, in *Fihi ma-Fihi*, explains it like this: God is like a baker: a baker needs for people to be hungry, otherwise he could not sell his bread; but he also wants people to be well fed, otherwise he would not feed them. Or God is like a doctor: he needs for there to be sick people, otherwise he could not pursue his profession; but he also wants people to be healthy, otherwise he would not heal them.

There is also a Nasrudin story which deals with the apparent ambiguities of Justice. God's perfect Justice is not always visible to us, since our perception is limited to time; but God's Knowledge is eternal:

> Once Hoja Nasrudin went to the Turkish bath. He was dressed in cheap, shabby clothes, so the attendants were not very excited about serving him; they handed him old towels and a thin scrap of the soap. But when he left, they were amazed when he presented each of them with a gold coin.
>
> A few days later he returned, this time dressed in magnificent robes. 'If this wealthy man tipped us so handsomely last time' the attendants thought, 'if we now attend him as he deserves, he will probably be even more generous.' So they treated him like a king. But when Nasrudin left the bath, he handed each of them a copper penny. Seeing their puzzled looks, he explained: 'The pennies are for *last* time. The gold coins were for *this* time.'

In the words of the Prophet, peace and blessings be upon him, 'His Throne is upon the waters, and in His other hand is the Balance (Justice), and He raises and lowers (whomever He will).'

> *Beware of oppressing someone with*
> *no defense against you except God.*
>
> —Hazrat 'Ali

X

DIGNITY
(*WAQAR; KARAMAH*)
THE SYNTHESIS
OF THE VIRTUES

O Muslims! Your blood, your property
and your honor are sacred to one another.
—Prophetic Hadith

Whoever feels his dignity decreasing
will see his enemy's strength growing.
—Hazrat 'Ali

IT IS DIFFICULT, in a way, to talk about the Dignity of the Prophet Muhammad, peace and blessings be upon him. His Dignity does not 'stand out' as an isolated trait because Dignity is the central virtue to which all other virtues pay tribute. There is no facet of his character which does not exemplify it. His Dignity is the Dignity of man in the presence of God. But if there was any moment in the Prophet's life when his Dignity was fully manifest, it was during his last pilgrimage, on the occasion of his Farewell Address:

After the principle rites had been completed the Prophet climbed to the summit of Mt. 'Arafa and preached from his camel to the multitude: After praising God, he said: 'Hear me, O people, for I do not know if I shall ever meet with you in this place again.' He exhorted them to treat one another well and reminded them of what was permitted and what was forbidden. Finally he said: 'I have left among you that which, if you hold fast to it, shall preserve you from all error, a clear indication, the Book of Allah and the word of his Prophet. O people, hear my words and understand!' Then he imparted to them a revelation which had just come to him, the last revelation of the Qur'an [or as some maintain, the second-to-last]: 'This day I have perfected for you your religion and fulfilled my favor unto you and chosen for you as your religion *al-Islam*.' (Q 5:3) He ended by asking twice: 'O people, have I fulfilled my mission?' A great cry of assent arose from the many thousands assembled on the lower slopes and at the foot of the hill. As he came down the hillside the last rays of the setting sun caught his head and shoulders; then darkness fell. Islam had been established and would grow into a great tree sheltering far greater multitudes.[1]

Dignity, however, does not first and foremost have to do with how we appear to others. When the Prophet was alone in the cave on Mt. Hira, did he lose his Dignity? Some authorities have spoken highly of solitude. According to Hatim al-Asamm, 'The believer loves solitude and isolation, while the hypocrite loves company and assemblies.' Yet Islam, more perhaps than any other religion except Judaism, emphasizes the need to relate to the community of believers. Though the Prophet thought highly of the Christian monks he encountered, he made it clear that there is no monasticism in Islam; 'each believer is a mirror to the others.' While those who are undergoing intensive spiritual training may be directed by their teacher to go into retreat for a time, the more central ideal is 'solitude in company', where fellowship is balanced by circumspection and discretion. The ultimate effect of this balance is to unify the character so that our behavior, except for necessarily private activities, is the same whether we are in company or alone. Dhu l'Nun al-Misri said: 'A person who does in secret what he would be ashamed to do in public has no self-respect; in fact, he does not even consider himself a living being.' Dignity, in Islam, is inseparable from Courtesy and Justice in our dealings with others. It is a social virtue. But this does

---

1. Charles Le Gai Eaton, *Islam and the Destiny of Man*, p128.

not mean that it is mere worldly 'respectability'. To practice Dignity is to protect, in the midst of social relations and activities, one's secret relationship with God.

In Islam it is still possible, so to speak, to stand as Adam before God; in the words of the prophetic *hadith*, 'Verily God created Adam in His own image.' Islam is the religion of the *fitrah*, our original human nature; it recognizes that, somewhere in each man and woman, the state of Adam and Eve before the fall still exists; it only needs to be awakened. In Christianity, especially western Christianity (Eastern Orthodoxy is somewhat closer to the Islamic position), the human nature is seen as fundamentally corrupted by sin, and God's redemptive act as a kind of infinite condescension—the restoration, through divine self-sacrifice, of a human Dignity irretrievably lost. In Islam, our *fitrah* is not and never can be lost; it is merely buried. The mirror of our original nature is tarnished and encrusted by *ghaflah*, heedlessness. It is polished, and returned to its original purity, by *dhikr*, the Remembrance of God. To stand as Adam or Eve before God is to stand in one's primordial human Dignity.

According to the Qur'an, *They have forgotten God, and so God has caused them to forget themselves* (59:19). In English, the phrase 'to forget yourself' means to engage in some kind of compulsive behavior that compromises your Dignity. In any society which has forgotten God, human Dignity becomes impossible without a conscious rejection of the norms of that society. If we see security, pleasure and power the final ends of human life, then we have no Dignity. If we identify with our desires for these things, if we define ourselves solely in terms of them, then we have forgotten ourselves in their presence. We have become two-dimensional, a caricature or cartoon of a human being; in the words of the Qur'an, *Shall I show you one who makes desire his god?* (25:43). The person who worships security we call 'coward', the one who worships pleasure a 'libertine', and the one who makes power his god a 'tyrant'. None of these three 'religions' support, or understand, human Dignity; the tyrant, the libertine, the coward are not complete human beings, except in essence. In terms of realization, they are merely fragments of the human form, even though they wear clothes and walk upright. The tyrant, the libertine, the coward are called to be *khalifa*, the viceregent of God on earth, but they have not heeded that call; they have betrayed the human trust.

Democracy in the west began as an assertion of universal human Dignity against the rule of tyrants. Dignity is not the sole possession of the king, the aristocrat, the rich man; every human being, simply by being human, possesses a share of that Dignity. In the words of Scottish poet Robert Burns, 'A man's a man for 'a that.' The 'revolution' of Muhammad, peace and blessings be upon him, was also democratic, in the sense that it overturned the hereditary power of the aristocracy and made provision for the poor one of the five pillars of Islam. But unlike the secular democratic revolutions of the west, it was based on a true understanding of human Dignity in terms of humanity's *khalifate*, our position as God's fully-empowered representative on earth. In Islam, our human Dignity is inherent, and inseparable from our essential humility, since we are also *'abd*, God's slave. And because we are slaves of God alone in our human essence, where our true Dignity is rooted—though not necessarily in our outer social relations, where we are necessarily beholden to others—it follows that, in our soul, in our human essence, we can be the slave of no man.

It is not society, however, that gives us our Dignity—not even religious society. Dignity, like every virtue, is part of our *fitrah*. If we live up to it, it blesses us; if we betray it, we earn its curse. Many today have a hard time understanding the concept of Dignity; they mistake it for pompousness or vanity. But humility too can be dignified. As American poet Lew Welch said, describing a Japanese Zen master: 'Suzuki bows with so much confidence we all feel bold.' Dignity makes no difference between myself and another; if a difference is made, it is the other who makes it. In the words of an obscure Catholic priest, speaking in the 1960s: 'True pride and true humility are the same thing.' So Dignity is the same as self-respect. Those who respect themselves will respect others; those who have no self-respect will despise others because they despise themselves. Dignity, unlike pompousness and vanity, is not based on other people's opinion of you—or on your opinion of yourself, for that matter. It has to do with being who God made you to be, irrespective of appearances.

Dignity is inseparable from Courage, Courtesy, Humility, and Justice; it does not try to make others feel undignified, but invites them to participate in the common Dignity of the human form. Powerfully and silently, it calls those who encounter it to awaken to their *fitrah*, their primordial human nature. Once upon a time, a traveler in the American southwest visited the country of the Hopi Indians, where he was introduced to a man of the tribe. His first condescending impression of this man was that he was nothing, really, but a poor Indian—ignorant, underprivileged, living in difficult and primitive conditions, without the blessings of modern civilization; the visitor 'looked down on him'. As he gazed at the man, however, he realized that the Hopi had not responded to his impression of him in any way, either by abasing himself or by standing up for himself. Usually when we look down on someone, he or she will sense it and react. This man did not. He was simply there. This impassiveness on the part of the Hopi began to impress the visitor, who now began to see him as exalted somehow, a sage, a 'noble savage,' perhaps even a saint. He started to 'look up' at the Indian instead of down on him. Where at first he had felt superior to him, he now felt and inferior and inadequate. But once again, the Hopi did not react. He neither expanded in response to the visitor's positive opinion of him, 'lording it over' him, nor did he modestly try to counteract that opinion. He was simply there. Finally the visitor's intensely positive impression began to moderate, till finally he, too, was simply there. He was no longer a 'privileged, educated American' nor an 'effete, over-protected American.' He was nothing but a man, standing with another man on the common earth. It was only his ego that had suffered inflation and deflation; his *fitrah* had not. Unlike the American—at least as he was at the beginning of the story—The Hopi remembered his Creator, and so knew his place in the universe. The 'moral' of this tale is that if we forget God, our psyche will wander aimlessly, while if we remember Him, we will rest in our true place; this is what it means to have Dignity.

So the root of Dignity is the remembrance of God. If we have forgotten ourselves because we have forgotten Him, only the remembrance of Him can restore that dignity and self-remembrance. Some have claimed that the practice of remembering God is none other than the practice of remembering ourselves; to be careful of our thoughts, our actions, our words and our physical motions and postures is seen as a way of standing consciously, and with Dignity, in the sight of God. And certainly this idea has some truth to it. But it is even truer to say that we will ultimately be unable to remember ourselves unless we remember God first. Self-remembering is another name for self-respect, a self-respect which is inseparable from an ability to view ourselves 'disinterestedly', objectively. And only a consciousness of the Absolute Object can give us this ability. If we try to remember ourselves without Him, we will never find the way out of the circle of our subjective egotism; to set one part of our subjective psyche the task of observing and remembering the other part is like 'setting the fox to guard the henhouse.' It can only end in obsessive self-involvement, or in the mental illness known as 'narcissism.' But if we awaken to the fact that there is no god but God, and that He is The Omniscient, the All-Seeing, the Universal Witness, the Knower of Each Separate Thing, the Totally Aware, then, knowing ourselves to be seen, we will see ourselves within the circle of His seeing; as God has said, *Remember Me and I will remember you.* (Q 2:152) And if we know that we are in the presence of the King, who has appointed us viceroy over this earthly reality, then we will carry ourselves with grace and dignity, humility and self-respect; we will live up to our *khalifate*; we will be faithful to the Trust.

> *God is Beautiful and loves Beauty.*
> —Prophetic Hadith

XI

THE PERFECTION
OF VIRTUE:
BEYOND THE
GREATER *JIHAD*

THE PRIMACY OF INTENT

CENTRAL TO ISLAMIC ETHICS is the principle, from the words of the Prophet, that 'acts are judged by their intent.' The person who thinks he can purify his intent without obeying moral rules is a fool, but the one who meticulously obeys moral rules only to avoid having to purify his intent is a hypocrite. A religion with a fully-developed sacred law covering all aspects of life would become stifling and pharisaical if the mystery of the human conscience were not given equal recognition. The following story, a different version of which appears in the *Mathnawi* of Jalalu'd-din Rumi, illustrates this principle:

> Once upon a time Moses encountered a shepherd, whose idea of worshipping God was to comb His hair, wash His feet and give Him milk to drink. The prophet thundered against the shepherd for dragging God down to the human level: 'Far be it from Him to need His hair combed! God is Lord of the Worlds; He is infinitely beyond your paltry conception of His Majesty. Rectify your practice, then. Worship Him in Spirit, not in form.' But as Moses traveled on, God came to him in a vision and chastised him: 'My servant the shepherd worshipped me according to his

conception—as do you. You have misjudged him; his sincerity is perfect in My sight.' Distraught and repentant, Moses ran back to the shepherd to ask his forgiveness. 'I beg your pardon, shepherd, for God has revealed to me that I had seriously misjudged you. Please continue to worship Him as seems right to you.' 'But I was about to thank you for your instruction!' the shepherd answered. 'The shock you administered opened my eyes to a vastly greater conception of God than the one I had previously held. After what I have seen, I can never return to my former practice.'

For us to be faithful to the religion of Islam, two things are needed: We must conform ourselves to the Islamic tradition, and we must allow the tradition to be born anew within us, in a unique way that is proper to us alone. If God, Who is *Al-Wahid*, The Unique, had not wanted each of us to realize Islam in his or her own unique way, He would not have made each of us different from all the others. In that timeless time before we were brought into existence, when God asked us *Am I not your Lord?* and we answered *Yea!* (Q 7:127), in that very instant each of us consented to be precisely who He made us to be—as if each of us, in a sense, were the reflection of a unique Name of God. We study the lives of great exemplars of virtue so that they can throw light on our own lives, not so that our unique talents and weaknesses and needs and capacities can be blotted out in the blinding light of the Hero. It is said that no one reaches God on his own feet, that to come to His threshold we must walk on God's feet. But it is equally true to say that no one can reach that threshold on the feet of someone else; if we aspire to step into God's shoes, it must be with our own feet. The character of the Prophet, peace and blessings be upon him, is so wide and so fully human that nothing we can express of the human soul, if it is expressed with Veracity, Sincerity, Courage and Submission to God, can really depart from the norm he embodies—as long as we remember that this expression is perfected not by breaking the outer forms of Islam, but by widening them within, until we realize that nothing that is truly alive in human life is excluded by them, only that which is decadent, subhuman and lifeless.

Those who worship their own uniqueness and originality instead of God are idolaters; but those who suppress this uniqueness so they can pour themselves blindly into an external mold have cheated God, who demands from us who we really are, not that lifeless thing we had hoped to become by denying and betraying who we are. Our uniqueness is not to be flaunted vainly before the eyes of the world; neither is it to be withheld from That One who has sought it out from all eternity.

BEYOND THE GREATER JIHAD

The greater *jihad* is the war between the Spirit (*al-Ruh*) and the commanding self (*al-nafs al-ammara*) for possession of the Heart (*al-Qalb*), the Center of consciousness and intent, the organ or power within the human being which is capable of direct knowledge of God.

The development of the virtues constitutes the entire strategy and tactics of the greater *jihad*.

The virtues develop through three stages:

1) *Knowing* what is right;

2) *Doing* what is right (this is *islam*, submission);

3) *Loving to do* what is right (this is *iman*, faith).

We *know* what is right from the Qur'an, the *hadith*, the *shari'ah*, from consulting legitimate religious authorities, and through praying to God for guidance. The faculties by which we know what is right, except in the case of prayer, are the *rational intellect* (*'aql*) and the *memory*.

We *do* what is right through the *will* (*irada*)—but only when it follows the rational intellect.

We *love to do* what is right through the *feelings*—but only when they follow the will.

This is how it is while the war between the Spirit and the commanding self is still going on. But after the war is won, after the Spirit takes full possession of the city of the Heart, the tactics and strategy of spiritual warfare are no longer necessary: the greater *jihad* is finished.

On the field of virtue, we *know* what is right through the rational intellect and memory, *do* what is right through the will, and *love to do* what is right through the feelings—when they are in line with and supportive of the will. But when the Heart is fully realized, when the Eye of the Heart is open, we no longer have to pass through these stages, because, in the city of the Heart, emotions, will and mind are one. It's not that we know what is right and then do it—it's that we have *become* rectitude. This is *ihsan*, excellence or perfection.

The Heart is a level *qualitative consciousness* that is inseparable from *spontaneous right action*. We no longer have to study what is right, plan our actions on the basis of this study, and then finally act, because knowledge, action and love now form an indivisible whole. Our character has become unified. We are no longer at war with ourselves. We have realized the self-at-peace. The Prophet Muhammad, peace and blessings be upon him, did not have to consult the Qur'an in every case before acting. As his wife A'isha said, when asked what the Prophet's character was like: 'His character was exactly like the Qur'an.' And the same is true of those friends of God whose wills are perfectly submitted to Him—though on a vastly different scale, because no saint can equal a prophet, and Muhammad was the last of the prophets. In other words, direct guidance, though answered prayer, is still possible. But it is certainly *not* possible for those who wish to rely upon such guidance alone, and ignore God's word as revealed in the Holy Qur'an. As the Prophet said, peace and blessings be upon him, 'Enter houses by their doors.'

The rational intellect, the will and the feelings are not annihilated in the Heart, but remain as servants of it. And one of the results of this servanthood is that the rational intellect no longer depends upon the memory. It now takes its cues from the Heart directly. The rational intellect on its own can never reach certainty, but it can *serve* certainty. Its role is to reveal the many different implications of what is already *certainly* known: either through revelation (*tanzil*)—the Holy Qur'an—or, by direct divine guidance, through the Heart.

But the Heart does not always act through its servants; sometimes it acts from its own indwelling Knowledge and Power—which is to say, by God's command. In the Qur'an this state is expressed by the verse *You did not throw when you threw, but God threw* (8:17), referring to the Prophet's act of throwing a handful of pebbles in the direction of the enemy at the battle of Badr, after which the tide turned in favor of the Muslims. It's as if his feelings were entirely absorbed into his will, his will into his rational intellect, and his rational intellect into the Heart. When the Heart acts at the command of God in such a way that the rational intellect, the will and the feelings no longer appear as separate stages of a process, then Unity of Character has been established. It's a little like what happens in the process of learning an art—calligraphy, for example. At the beginning we must consciously practice, study various styles, learn from our mistakes—but at the end, we no longer have to painstakingly direct our hand to do what our memory tells us to do, because we have *become* calligraphy.

Only someone with Unity of Character can hope to have the capacity to directly witness, not simply believe in, the Unity of God. For those who have attained this Unity, the greater *jihad* has come to a triumphant close upon their entry into *dar es-Salaam*, the Abode of Peace.

XII

THE ROLE OF ROMANCE
IN CHARACTER-
DEVELOPMENT

Three things have been made delightful to me:
women, perfume, and prayer.
—Prophetic Hadith

THE FIRST MOVE in the greater *jihad* — the war against the passions of the *nafs al-ammara* or 'commanding self' — is to establish obedience to the *shari'ah*. The second is to develop the virtues, and gain insight into them. But while carrying on the work of conforming our souls to virtue, we also need to take a look at the 'raw material' the virtues must form and redeem.

Intense emotion, especially erotic emotion, is close to the well-springs of our life. Passionate emotion is like fire: If no limits are set to it, it will destroy everything it touches. But if the fire of life is allowed to go out, or if it is buried so far underground that we can no longer use it, then both our emotions and our perceptions will become cold and contracted; if we fail to feel, we will also fail to know. We will find it harder to obtain good emotional nourishment, and we ourselves will remain 'uncooked.' Someone with an unrefined, undeveloped character is called 'raw'; someone who has indulged his or her passions until nothing left is called 'burnt out'. The idea is neither to stay raw nor to become burnt-out, but rather to be *well-cooked*, so that other people can 'savor' our character. (The ego, on the other hand, needs to be reduced to ashes in the

Fire of God; the ash of the ego is the most potent fertilizer for the soul's garden.)

The fire of passion needs to be curbed by the virtues; yet this fire, in the form of Hope, Striving, Zeal, Aspiration, and Loving-kindness, is the very force needed to develop the entire spectrum of the virtues; it is the source of their power. The virtues are not empty shells which have no purpose but to protect us from outside contamination; they are more like cooking-utensils filled with good, solid nourishment.

In order to acquire the virtues, we must encounter the passions—not all the passions nor every degree of them, but only the ones God has destined us to encounter for the development of our character. On one occasion in the 1960s, somewhere in the United States, two spiritual seekers sat talking together. The first seeker preached the value of overcoming egotism, of renouncing desire. The second replied: 'But that's not my problem. Before I transcend passion and renounce desire, first I'll have to *find* them. How grateful I would be if I could really desire *anything* whole-heartedly.' On two occasions, before his marriage, the Prophet, peace and blessings be upon him, was tempted to taste the vices of Makkan nightlife; on both occasions, God intervened between him and his lower desires. It was only then that the virtue of Chastity latent in him was made actual.

We all desire many things, both positive and negative, both material and spiritual. But if there is a single experience which gathers together in one place all our scattered, lost, repressed and dissipated desires, it is passionate human love. Human love, and especially erotic love—if, that is, our beloved is truly worthy: self-respecting, generous without being promiscuous, and with a strong and beautiful character—must call upon Courage, Courtesy, Vigilance, Self-denial, Self-sacrifice, Generosity, Trustworthiness, Humility, Mercy: any virtue you could name. An unworthy object, on the other hand, will either not call up all the virtues, or will ultimately lead us to squander and degrade them . . . though if we wake up in time, even an unworthy beloved can teach us a great deal—which, of course, is no excuse for seeking out the unworthy. (In the words of the Qur'an, *God is the best of plotters*; sometimes He leads us astray in order to guide us. Let us pray that we remain open to that guidance, so that we do not go astray forever!)

But just because the virtues have been called up, they will not necessarily appear in well-developed form. And since undeveloped virtues cannot be relied upon, the corresponding vices will appear as well, tempting us to reach the goal by dishonorable methods because the virtuous methods apparently haven't worked: not lust alone, but also fawning, hypocrisy, bribery, deception, intimidation, as well as negative emotions like despondency, giddiness, jealousy, anger and suspicion. In addition to our potential or actual virtues, a human beloved will inevitably confront us with all our shortcomings, attachments, and vanities. And human beloveds have one serious drawback: though we may catch the scent of eternal love by means of our love for them, they themselves are not eternal: *All is perishing except His Face.*

But in a culture of sexual promiscuity and de-emphasis of sexual differences—which, surprisingly, seem to go together—sexual desire is split off from romantic love. It becomes hard to love anyone deeply and passionately enough to transform one's soul. In the Arabic *udhri* poems of the early Islamic period which celebrated unrequited 'platonic' love, and in the troubadour poems of southern France which are descended from them (the word 'troubadour' comes from the Arabic for 'player of the *ribab*'); in the poetry of Hafiz, in the Persian romances *Yusuf and Zulaikha* (Jami), *Layla and Majnun* (Nizami) and others, and in many of the Romances of King Arthur from France, Britain and Germany, the whole point of the story is that the beloved is *difficult to win*. The lover becomes mad, goes into exile, suffers in body and spirit, and often even dies before he can reach her (or him). In some stories he does win her; in others, the completion of their love is reserved for the world to come.

In these times, however, we find it progressively harder to understand and believe in this kind of love. If beloved number one is hard to get, we say to ourselves, then why not simply go after beloveds two, three and four? As the English saying goes, 'there are plenty of fish in the sea.' 'Difficult' now means 'undesirable;' in cultures of promiscuity, our desires are directed only toward what is easy to get;

we are expected to be 'of easy virtue'—a phase which used to be applied particularly to immoral women. In the realm of love between the sexes the person we love is no longer *worth* waiting for, suffering for, making sacrifices for. They are no longer *dear* to us (an English synonym for 'expensive'). Nor are we ourselves content to wait until someone comes along who values us highly and is willing and able to prove it. We have let ourselves become 'cheap'. The reason for this is that modern cultures have lost the virtue of Modesty or Shame. Modesty protects our erotic and romantic feelings from being wasted on unworthy objects, polluted by vice and vanity, or eaten up by motives of worldly power.

What *prodigality* is to money, *promiscuity* is to sex. When our sexuality and romantic feelings are kept pure, they remain powerful. When they are squandered and polluted, they become weakened, jaded, effete. Wendy Shalit, in her book *A Return to Modesty*,[1] describes the effect of the death of Modesty in America and Europe, and the reasons some women are returning to it. These reasons fall short of religion, but they are clearly moving in a religious direction:

> We thought we could have everything and everyone, and really we came up with nothing. 'If it feels good, do it,' was the motto of the sixties, and after we did it, we found that it no longer felt good. We thought that giving up extra-erotic considerations [in relationships between the sexes] would liberate the erotic, but in fact it spoiled it entirely. [p191]

> The persistence of sexual modesty challenges and ultimately refutes the equation of the libertine with the erotic, because those who are returning to virtue are doing so for precisely sensual reasons. They are often totally secular, but have found vice boring and insipid.

> Modesty is the proof that morality is sexy.

> It may even be the proof of God, because it means that we have been designed in such a way that when we humans act like

---

1. Wendy Shalit, *A Return to Modesty: Discovering the Lost Virtue* (New York: Simon and Schuster, 1999).

animals, without any restraint and without any rules, we just don't have as much fun. [pp192–193]

According to the German poet Ranier Maria Rilke, love is difficult, and ought to be; nothing of any worth can be attained in life except through difficulty. And the same is true in the spiritual life: God is the most difficult to win of all beloveds, which might lead us to despair, except that He is also the most generous and the most merciful. This is why the difficulty of winning the human beloved often becomes, in romantic literature of both east and west, a symbol of the difficulty—or rather the impossibility—of gaining access to God through our own efforts, apart from His Mercy. Yet these efforts still must be made. According to the Muslim proverb, 'not everyone who hunts zebra catches one, but anyone who catches a zebra has to have hunted them first.' In the words of Frithjof Schuon,

> All great spiritual experiences agree in this: there is no common measure between the means put into operation and the result. With men this is impossible, but 'With God all things are possible,' says the Gospel. In fact, what separates man from divine Reality is the slightest of barriers; God is infinitely close to man, but man is infinitely far from God. This barrier, for man, is a mountain; man stands in front of a mountain which he must remove with his own hands. He digs away the earth, but in vain, the mountain remains; man however goes on digging in the name of God. And the mountain vanishes. It was never there.[2]

In many medieval romances, both Muslim and Christian, the beloved can only be won after overcoming dangerous trials, like digging through a mountain with your bare hands, trials which often include slaying a monster or a dragon or an evil knight. It's as if a kind of adulterous love-triangle exists between a Princess, a Dragon who keeps her captive, and a Hero who rescues her. (The Greek myth of Perseus and Andromeda and the sea monster Cetus is perhaps the earliest version of this story.) One way we can look at

2. Frithjof Schuon, *Stations of Wisdom* (Bloomington, IN: World Wisdom Books, Inc., 1995), p157.

stories like this is as a picture of what is going on in our own inner world. From this point of view, the Hero is our will and rational intelligence in service to our conscience or 'accusing self', trying their best to follow what seems to be true and worthy, fighting against everything low and false, and sometimes going mad in the process. (Madness symbolizes the intuition of a Reality higher than conscious will and rational intelligence.) The Dragon is our passions, our unconscious ego, the 'commanding self' which holds our soul, the Princess, in bondage. (In Nizami's romance of *Layla and Majnun*, the 'dragon' appears, at one point, as Layla's family, who want to keep the lovers separated because they see Majnun's love-madness as socially shameful and dishonorable.) And the Princess, rescued from the commanding self, is the 'self-at-peace,' our power to submit, in 'unadulterated' purity, to the Will of God.

Make no mistake: Flirting with sinful behavior is never justified. But the fact remains that—unless we are under God's rarest kind of protection—sinful behavior will flirt with *us*: so we'd better be ready for it. And if we are unaware of the nature and condition of our *nafs*, we will not be ready for it. Every passion is a perversion of a God-given human faculty. If we deny ourselves conscious knowledge of the state of our own faculties, hoping that this will save them from perversion, then we have rejected 'O God, show me things as they really are,' and built our spiritual lives on a very shaky foundation. Nonetheless, we can never know our passions as they really are unless we resist their demands; only a serious and balanced asceticism can *concretely* and *experientially* demonstrate the difference between the demands of the *nafs al-ammara* (which loves nothing better than to masquerade as religious piety, to portray anger as zeal and lust as spiritual intoxication) and God's true commands. Our passions—lust, anger and all the rest—are the excess or residue in our psyches of the vast overflow of God's general and creating Mercy, *al-Rahman*—the very powers He uses to create and maintain the universe. And this is precisely why—when dedicated to *al-Rahim*, God's particular and saving Mercy, manifesting as prophecy, religion and sacred law—they are the very *virtue* or *potency* that allows us to follow the norms of religion in the fullness, and the *gladness*, of submission.

IF WE ARE dedicated to Truth, *Al-Haqq*, then emotion itself can be a step on the way to Truth; if our will is constant in obedience to God, our feelings will eventually follow, to strengthen and refine our efforts and help them ripen into wisdom. Our feelings may even have turned to God before our will has truly chosen Him; but without the firm dedication of the will, this feeling-for-God can never be stable. It may even fool us into thinking we are intimate with Him, when all we are doing is turning our fantasies of God into a form of entertainment or self-reassurance. Yet our feelings can also make a sincere appeal to our will, in these terms: 'Come and take full responsibility for what we can only dream of—the constant remembrance of God.' As one contemporary authority has written:

> It is habitually assumed in today's world that feeling is strictly subjective. But it is more accurate to say that some feelings are objectively true and others objectively false. If you love a demon, for example, your feelings are not *true*. The modern world revels in the passions, but in many ways it attempts to kill the 'still, small voice' of objective feeling. True feeling can often seem small and unimportant, like alpine flowers, even though these seemingly insignificant plants have the power to endure great cold. . . . There are certain avenues to the transcendent Intellect which are only open through feeling.[3]

All true love, whether of a human beloved or of the All-Merciful and All-Compassionate, requires a death. The relationship between love and death is succinctly expressed in this poem by the Andalusian poet Abu-l-Hasan Ibn al-Qabturnuh (Lysander Kemp's translation):

I remembered Sulayma when the passion
   of battle was as fierce
As the passion of my body when we parted.

I thought I saw, among the lances, the tall
   perfection of her body,
And when they bent toward me I embraced them.

---

3. Jennifer Doane Upton, 'High Romance and the Spiritual Path', unpublished.

This is the essence of the romantic sensibility in two stanzas. There is always something excessive and unbalanced in the romantic view of life; yet a heart which is entirely closed to romance is itself unbalanced, and in need of 'moistening.' We need to prune our roses, but we also need to water them.

In the romantic view of life there is a kind of confusion of levels. The beauty that belongs to Paradise alone breaks through into this world, and this is undeniably a part of the great generosity of God. Yet if we make idols out of those forms, limited in space and cut short by time, which the grace of Paradise has touched—and it seems we always do—we will also experience a foretaste of the fires of hell.

All this is to teach us and guide us. If God never showed Himself as *Al-Wadud*, The Loving-kind, in this world of passing forms, if He never appeared dramatically and romantically in the events of our lives, He might never become real to us. Romance sees the youths and maidens of Paradise on the dusty roads of this world; but this is not their home. Heaven and earth cannot contain the Beloved, but the Heart can. And when we truly come to know this, then the drama of love and war which is the essence of romance, and which we project on the impoverished screen of this world, breaks camp, packs its bags, and returns to the Heart where it began, leaving behind it nothing but the ashes of dead campfires. The Heart knows that the death required by love is not ultimately of the body, or of this or that outer enemy, but of the ego itself. In the contest for the true Beloved, the *nafs al-ammara* is the only rival.

After the Prophet, peace and blessings be upon him, returned to Madinah from his last pilgrimage, he did not have long to live.

When he returned to the wife whose day it was—for he was meticulous in apportioning his time—he asked her, 'Where am I tomorrow?' She told him which wife he was due to visit. 'And the day after tomorrow?' Struck by his insistence, she realized that he was impatient to be with 'A'isha and went at once to speak with the others. They came to him together and said: 'O Messenger of Allah, we have given our days with you to our sister 'A'isha,' and he accepted the gift. But 'A'isha was suffering from a headache, groaning 'Oh my head.' 'No,' he said, with a last glint of humour, 'No, 'A'isha—*my* head!'. . . .

On 12 Rabi'u'l-awwal in the eleventh year of the Hijra, which in the Christian calendar is 8 June 632, he entered the mosque for the last time. Abu Bakr was leading the prayer, and he motioned to him to continue. He watched the people, his face radiant. 'I never saw the Prophet's face more beautiful than it was at that hour,' said his friend Anas. Returning to 'A'isha's apartment he laid his head on her breast. He had used the last of his strength and soon after lost consciousness.

She thought this was the end, but after an hour or so he opened his eyes and she heard him murmur: 'With the supreme communion in Paradise....': or perhaps he had said: 'With the companions....' These were his last words. His head grew heavy on the girl's breast, and when she was sure that he was gone, she laid him gently down and rose to express her sorrow and the people's sorrow in the accustomed ways, breaking death's silence with the cries which expose all human grief to the earth and the sky and the four corners of the world.[4]

> *But such as fears the Station of his Lord,*
> *for them shall be two gardens—*
> *O which of your Lord's bounties will you and you deny?*
> *therein two fountains of running water—*
> *O which of your Lord's bounties will you and you deny?*
> *reclining upon couches lined with brocade—*
> *O which of your Lord's bounties will you and you deny?*
> *therein maidens restraining their glances,*
> *untouched before them by any man or jinn—*
> *O which of your Lord's bounties will you and you deny?*
> *lovely as rubies, beautiful as coral—*
> *O which of your Lord's bounties will you and you deny?*
> *Shall the recompense of goodness be other than goodness?*
>
> —Qur'an 55:46–60

---

4. Charles Le Gai Eaton, *Islam and the Destiny of Man*, p 129

TAFSIR OF
THE HOLY QUR'AN

TAFSIR OF
THE HOLY QUR'AN

IF, AS A'ISHA SAID, the character of the Prophet Muhammad, peace and blessings be upon him, was just like the Qur'an, we can learn more about him by a deep reading of the Holy Book—and more about the Book through meditating on the Prophet's character: each is a mirror for the other.

Everything in all the worlds is reflected, in one way or another, in the Holy Qur'an. There is the Qur'an which God sent down to inspire and warn and guide us, *in the clear Arabic tongue*; there is also the Qur'an which God keeps to Himself—not because He is not Generous, but because mankind is not great enough or wise enough to read it. This Qur'an is 'the Mother of the Book'; it is God's knowledge of the universe He creates *with naught but Truth*, which is too vast for us to understand. And if, once in a while, we catch a momentary glimpse of it, it is entirely due to God's Mercy, not our own cleverness.

God has many Names; likewise the Qur'an has many levels of meaning. One of God's Names is *al-Batin*, the Inner; another is *al-Zahir*, the Outer. Both are reflected in the Qur'an, which means that some levels of its meaning will be more inward, others more outward. *Both are essential.* The more inner meanings do not deny the outer, but show us the deeper significance of the outer. In the same way, the more outer meanings do not deny the inner, but show us how the inner significance should take its place in our daily lives and actions. When the Qur'an directs us to pray every day, we pray. God is Lord, we are servants, and through the Qur'an comes the law. Yet the Qur'an also says, *the Remembrance of God is greater* than prayer. Does this mean that as long as we remember God we don't have to pray? Certainly not. It means that our prayer should not become mechanical, that the inner reason for prayer is to help us remember God—and that the remembrance of God is something deeper than the actions of our body and the words of our mouth; *because* it is deeper than they are, it expresses itself *through* them. There is no heart without a body; by the same token, there is no body without a heart.

The written Qur'an is the body; the Qur'an being recited is the breath and life of the body; the meaning of the Qur'an is the Heart.

THE FAMILY OF ʿIMRAN, 3

Step by step He has sent down to you this book,
setting forth the truth which confirms
whatever remains of earlier revelations:
for it is He who earlier bestowed from on high
the Torah and the Gospel, as a guidance to humankind,
and it is He who has bestowed the standard for discernment.

Here the Qur'an makes clear that it is not the exclusive revelation of God, only the final one, and also that it is the *standard of discernment* for what still remains uncorrupted of His earlier revelations to humanity. But this standard of discernment, this *furqan*, is also the spirit of God's Truth within us. If we accept the Qur'an, and follow it, and let it inform us—'form us within', that is—then our Heart, God willing, will ultimately become like a mirror, impartially reflecting things as they really are, without the rust and dents of our own subjectivity getting in the way. This mirror-like objectivity, this freedom from vice and passion and heedlessness, is the light by which we can discern the truth. In the words of Muhammad, peace and blessings be upon him, 'O Lord, show me things as they really are.'

But what does it mean that the Qur'an was sent down *step by step*? Was this simply a concession to the human limitations of the Prophet, or the imperfect receptivity of the community? Or does it have another meaning as well?

If Truth were to dawn upon us all at once, it would shatter us. Each revelation must be actualized before another is sent. And this is true both of God's great revelations to man which are the religions of the Book, and of his unveilings of Truth to the human Heart. If we have not finished the last job, a good employer will not load us with another, both because he does not want to overwork us, and because we must prove by finishing one task that we are capable of assuming another. One of the reasons the Qur'an was sent down step by step was to demonstrate that the spiritual life is a path composed of many steps. And just as one can only walk ten miles by covering those miles with many steps, one after the other, 'skipping' none of them, so the path of submission to God is arranged in various stages or stations. Repentance must come before trust-in-God, for example, since no one who trusts that his sins will advance or support or protect him in this world is ready to put his trust in his true Sustainer. Likewise *islam*—the willingness to follow the norms of the religion—must come before *iman*, deep faith, which itself must come before *ihsan*, excellence or perfection. And each of these stages or stations *confirms* the stations that went before; it strengthens and establishes them, and also shows exactly how they were the necessary preliminaries to what comes after. The Qur'an enters the heart of every believer in the same way as it was originally revealed to Muhammad: step by step.

SAD, 29

This Book of blessings We have sent down to you
so that they may meditate on its signs,
and that people of insight might take them to heart.

To *take . . . to heart* the signs of the Holy Qur'an is to let them enter and inform and purify the spiritual Heart within us. What our mind remembers and applies reason to, what our Heart ponders and understands, finally comes into union with what the Spirit of

God within us already knows. The Qur'an *is* that very Spirit refracted into words, like a prism refracts the light of the sun into many colors. And the Spirit, the Eye of the Heart, is both what allows us to understand the meaning of the Qur'an and *take [it] . . . to heart*, and the substance of the Qur'an itself before it comes into this world; in the mirror of the Qur'an the Spirit sees its own image. As we *meditate on its signs*, its words are transformed into meanings—and those meanings are finally united with the Source of all meaning, with the Truth itself.

THE THRONGS, 21–23

Truly in this is a Message of remembrance for people of insight.
Is one whose heart God has opened to surrender
so that he is illumined by a light from his Sustainer
no better than one who is hard-hearted?
Woe to those whose hearts are hardened
against remembrance of God!
They obviously wander astray!
God has revealed the most beautiful message
in the form of a Book consistent within itself,
repeating its teaching in various guises.
The skins of those who stand in awe of their Lord tremble with it;
then their skins and their hearts soften
with the remembrance of God.
Such is God's guidance:
with it He guides the one who wills to be guided,
but those whom God lets stray have none to guide them.

The Qur'an is addressed to our intelligence because it is composed of nothing but truth. But if our hearts are hard, we cannot hear this truth; our intelligence is darkened. Those whose hearts are hard see only the hard outer surface of things, the world of 'facts' or 'hard data'. The world of truths, of which all facts are illustrations, is closed to them. If all you can see are facts, not truths, the world you experience will have no unity to it. It will not be a universe, only a random collection of objects and details. And if you cannot see the unity of the universe, you will certainly not be able to see the unity of God's other Book, the Holy Qur'an; the fact that the Book repeats its teaching in various guises will seem to you like inconsistency.

All this changes, however, when we remember God. The sense of God's real presence puts us in a state of *awe*, and this awe opens us to understand the real meanings of the Qur'an. Those who can stand in *awe* of it will then be able to see the *beauty* of that *beautiful message*.

The remembrance of God *softens* our *skins* and our *hearts*. For our *skins* to be softened is for us to become sensitive, such that we allow things to *touch* us deeply. Those whose skins are softened are capable of being touched by people and things in the outer world, including the vocal recitation of the Qur'an. Those whose *hearts* are softened are capable of being touched by invisible, inner realities—the inner meanings of the Qur'an. They can see how the *various guises* of Qur'anic teaching are not opposed to its Unity, but are actually expressions of this Unity. And to know this about the Qur'an is to begin to know this about the universe, too. Each unique object that God has created, each unique event He causes to happen, is equally an expression of His Unity and His Truth. Only the Absolute Unity of God can embrace all the things and situations of our lives, so that each happening is a new sign, a new unfolding of the Reality of the One God.

The *one whose heart has opened to surrender . . . is illumined by a light from his Sustainer.* So *surrender* is the seed of intelligence, the door that admits the light of God to illuminate our hearts. There are some people who want to learn and memorize everything before putting *any* of it into practice; but these people are deluded. God is Reality, and those who do not completely surrender to Reality will never understand it. They will be lost in the maze of their own ideas and opinions. When an architect or an engineer designs a building or a machine according to the laws of physics, he or she is surrendering to Reality. The architect or engineer knows that if he does not follow these laws but instead ignores them or rebels against them, his knowledge will no longer be knowledge, only imagination; consequently his work will fail. Those who simply collect data about Reality are perhaps not entirely wasting their time, since one of the items of information they may run across is that there is no true realization without surrender. But then they have to *do it*. Academic religious studies may (or may not) give us knowledge *about* God, but only surrender, only *islam*, can give us knowledge *of* God. Without God's *guidance*, however, we cannot even surrender to Him; all we can do is *wander astray*. Our hearts will remain hard. So the first step is to seek that guidance, and then be willing to follow it wherever it leads.

IBRAHIM, 24–27

Are you not aware how God sets forth the parable of a good word?
It is like a good tree, firmly rooted, with its branches towards the sky,
yielding its fruit at all times by its Sustainer's permission.
And God propounds parables to men,
so that they might themselves reflect on the truth.
And the parable of a corrupt word is that of a corrupt tree,
torn up from its roots onto the face of the earth,
wholly unable to endure.
God grants firmness to those who have attained to faith
through the word that is unshakably true
in the life of this world as well as in the life to come.

THIS IS THE STORY of the destiny of a good word vs. a bad one. But whose word is it? Who, in these verses, is the speaker?

If *God grants firmness to those who have attained faith through the word that is unshakably true*, then the Speaker is God, and the unshakably true word is the Qur'an.

A word spoken by God is always true. Circumstances change, but God's word remains unshaken. When God's word takes root in the earth of the soul, it gives us a true ground to stand on, a strong foundation for our life. And it also gives us the ability to turn to the

Spirit of God for sustenance, like a tree receiving life-giving rain and the vivifying light of the sun. The earth in which the word takes root is the ground of virtue, particularly the virtues of spiritual poverty and humility. If we are willing to lower ourselves like the earth, we can receive God's word like the earth receives the seed. This lowness, this *humility* (from the Latin word *humus*, soil), is what allows our spiritual lives to grow toward the sun of the Spirit.

But if God is the One Who speaks the good word, then who speaks the corrupt word? We could say 'Eblis'; we could also say the *nafs al-ammara*, the commanding self. The commanding self believes, or acts as if it believes, that it exists in its own right. It thinks it can create reality out of nothing through its lies, its fantasies, and its schemes. But such 'co-creation' is simply not possible. *We created the heavens and the earth with naught but Truth*, but nothing whatever can be created out of lies and illusions, no matter how much effort we expend. Lies and illusions can certainly destroy (though not without God's permission, so He can demonstrate to us their consequences), but they can never create. They are neither rooted in the ground of trust and sincerity, nor can their branches reach upward to receive Life and Truth and Mercy from the Sustainer.

But we ourselves are also speakers. When God speaks, He creates; when we speak, we either conform ourselves to His creative Word, or we depart from it into a world of lies and illusions. To speak truth is to make truth our ally—both the simple factual truth, and that Truth which one of the Names of God Himself, *Al-Haqq*. The objective truth of any situation—not the lies we tell, or the way we hope it will be, or the way we fear it will be—is God's real presence in that situation. It may seem that liars have all power in this world, just as someone who has just jumped off a high cliff may feel that he is motionless and weightless. But truth will always have the final word, *in the life of this world as well as in the life to come*.

The human form stands upright like a tree. Only the human being is capable of being conscious of God's presence while remaining firmly rooted in this world. But if we fail to heed the true word, if we resort to lies and evasions, then we can depend neither upon the ground of the actual situation, nor upon the Truth and Mercy of God; we are *wholly unable to endure*.

Bismillah ar-Rahman ar-Rahim

This phrase, the *Basmalah*, begins the Qur'an, and every verse of the Qur'an except one. It is said to be the epitome of the Qur'an in a single verse. The Qur'an is often severe, since it was sent to save us, and in order to be saved we often need to be warned. But the Basmalah shows that the Qur'an is in essence a Mercy from God, and that Mercy is closer than wrath to God's true nature.

God has two mercies: *Rahman,* His general Mercy, by which He creates the universe, and *Rahim,* His particular Mercy, by which He leads all things back to Himself. By *Rahman,* He grants the wish of all possible things to be actualized; He bestows upon them the Life and Reality they long for. The joy of sexuality and the fear of death are the measure of the depth of this longing. But the desire for separate existence, which begins as a Mercy, ends under the sign of wrath: departing from God, or rather from the knowledge that God is the only Reality, created beings reach the outer darkness, subject to evils and sufferings of every kind, and they cry to God for relief. In response to this cry, God unveils *Rahim,* which manifests itself in terms of religions, and sacred laws, and prophets, and saints, and the *straight path.* All creation cries to be saved, and *Rahim* mercifully dawns to show the way back to God—the Sovereign Good—the only Reality.

The Mercy of creation is general because it encompasses all things. The Mercy of divine revelations such as the Qur'an is also general to a degree because it is addressed to an entire community; yet within it are the seeds of a particular Mercy, one addressed to 'myself' alone. And even though our work under the sign of *Rahim* is the 'war against the soul', the struggle to overcome the passions, which ends with 'die before you are made to die'—the annihilation of 'myself' as a separate and seemingly self-created entity—nonetheless, without the appearance of this 'myself', the spiritual crisis which announces the dawn of God's particular Mercy, and the ultimate return of all creation to Him, could not take place.

Religion is God's wish that we abandon exclusive attachment to His general and creating Mercy and commit ourselves to His particular and saving Mercy. Only humanity is confronted with this choice. The angels made their choice in pre-eternity, and those who have retained angelic status remain plunged in the contemplation of God. The animals, the plants, the minerals are fixed under *Rahman*; their purpose is fulfilled through their mere existence, while humanity's purpose is fulfilled only through our self-transcendence. Only humanity can consciously choose, by God's grace, to shift our center-of-gravity from *Rahman* to *Rahim*. So religion requires us to break identification with one of God's mercies and avail ourselves of the other. Of course *Rahman*, as God's universal Mercy, can never really be left behind, since it is by this Mercy that we exist. But we can leave behind our exclusive dependence upon natural good (which is how the stream of *Rahman* appears within the human psyche)—upon natural instinctive desires, that is, and the objects which fulfill them—and place our spiritual center in *Rahim*, in the religion which God has mercifully given to us as a way back to Him.

There is no evil in *Rahman*; existence itself, as free a gift of God to our own nothingness, is only good. Nonetheless, *Rahman* is what makes evil possible, which is why it is said in the Qur'an, *I seek refuge in the Lord of Daybreak from the evil of that which He created* (113:1–2). Whatever has departed from God into the world of separate existence is subject to all the limitations of that world, including the possibility of evil. And this, like everything else, is in line with God's will. If the world could exist as something other than God and still be perfect, it would be like a second God, which we know is impossible. Paradise is nearness to God, which is why it overflows with God's Mercy; this world, since it at a greater distance from God, must be mixed with God's wrath—which is also a sign of His Presence, although a negative one. All this is expressed in the Qur'anic verse *There is no refuge from God, but in Him* (9:118). If God had not created the universe by His general Mercy, His particular Mercy would have no field of operation—just as a salmon, though it must fight against the current to swim upstream, would have no river to travel in if the water were not flowing downstream. Both *Rahman* and *Rahim* are of God, but only *Rahim* leads to the return of all existing things to their Source in God.

In a way, God gives us only what we ask for. To those who desire Him above all else He gives Paradise; to those who desire above all else to flee from Him, via the distractions of the world and the enticements of the passions, He gives the Fire. And if it were somehow within the power of those in the Fire to desire Him more than they desire to flee from Him, it would certainly within His power to grant their wish.

Only God can claim for Himself the name 'Reality'; and since whatever is Real is necessarily Good, God is the source of both the Mercy of existence and Compassion for the suffering of existence. If we try to claim the name Reality for ourselves, we depart from Reality, and enter into the unreality of evil. If we approach Reality, and recognize that whatever Reality we have is not ours but His, we experience both the Mercy of His gift of Reality to us, and the Mercy of the return of this gift to the heart of Reality Itself. Within the inconceivable Unity of God, *Rahman* and *Rahim* are eternally and perfectly united, without the shadow of a distinction between them.

COUNSEL, 15

And so, call out to them
and stand steadfast as you have been commanded,
and do not follow their likes and dislikes, but say:
'I have faith in the Book which God has bestowed from on high;
and I am asked to judge justly between you.
God is our Sustainer and your Sustainer.
To us belongs the responsibility for our deeds, and to you, your deeds.
Let there be no argument between us and you.
God will bring us all together, and with Him is all journeys' end.'

Here Allah commands the Prophet not to run after all those whom he wants to influence, but to take his stand on the Truth, accepting those who come and not trying to entice the others by making the religion 'palatable' to them. *God lets go astray whom He wills, just as He guides unto Himself all who turn to Him* (Q 13:27). The power of

Truth is based on Truth itself, and on one's remaining faithful to it, not upon some attempt to 'tailor' it for this or that audience. To take one's stand on the Truth is to be filled with, and radiate, the power of the Truth. Certainly Allah 'tailored' the Qur'an for the people to whom it was addressed and the time in which it was revealed, as well as for all subsequent people who were destined to become Muslims in later times. But that was His right, not ours— not even Muhammad's. The 'uncreated' Qur'an, in the form of *Umm al-Kitab*, 'The Mother of the Book,' lives as an eternal expression of the secret essence of God. The Qur'an we can hold in our hands and read and recite is only that portion of the uncreated Eternal Qur'an which has come, still uncreated, into time. Within the created, temporal world, it stands as a sign of *al-Qayyum*, the Uncreated, and of *al-Samad*, the Eternal.

Since the Qur'an was sent to the Arabs, it was revealed in *the clear Arabic tongue* (Q 16:103); it cannot therefore be translated into any other tongue, and remain the Qur'an. This is a sign of the immutability of its essential message. Thus we could say that the Holy Qur'an represents Divine Objectivity. We usually think of the 'objective' world as the world of things, persons and situations we know through our senses. Your inner psychological world of thoughts and feelings changes with great rapidity—but the hill outside your window will still be there when the sun rises tomorrow. The word 'objective' makes us think of logic, rationality and a scientific outlook, whereas the word 'subjective' suggests either bias and inaccuracy, or a kind of 'tender,' artistic inner world of feeling and imagination.

What we don't always realize is that there is a higher objectivity than that of the material world; there is a science of spiritual things as well as a science of nature. God is eternal, and the higher worlds he has created—such as *malakut*, the subtle world, which is like the objective aspect of the world of dreams, or *jabarut*, the world of the spiritual intellect—are *relatively* eternal, which is to say they are eternal in relation to the world of matter. And whatever is eternal is *objective* in relation to things which change over time.

The Qur'an is a manifestation of a higher *spiritual objectivity*, uninfluenced both by our subjective moods and opinions, and by the instability and changefulness of the material world. This is why the Prophet is commanded by Allah to stand by his faith in the Book, and judge on that basis, not on the basis of his own likes and dislikes, or those of other people.

In the modern world, where many different religions are now available—especially in the West—people sometimes get the idea that they can choose which religion to follow based on their *preferences*. Religion is treated as a consumer product, like an automobile or a computer. If a particular religion gives someone a 'good feeling' the first time he investigates it, if he is 'comfortable' with it, then he believes it may be for him—until he encounters difficulties, that is, or until his preferences change. And many religious leaders present their religions in just this way; they pander to the popular taste. The idea that the religions are different versions of an objective spiritual Truth, sent by God to different nations at different times for His own purposes, is becoming progressively harder for people to understand. Religion is seen as something which *fulfills our needs*, not as a manifestation of God in this world which *requires something of us*—or rather, which requires everything.

God makes clear in these verses that the Prophet judges not on the basis of his own preferences, but on the basis of a Criterion by which he himself will also be judged. The existence of this objective Criterion takes things off the level of a struggle between 'my truth' and 'your truth', since both of us are judged by *the* Truth, and can turn toward that Truth whenever we face uncertainty. In the light of this Criterion—which is ultimately God Himself, as revealed through the Holy Qur'an—*the desire to be right* is transformed into *the desire to know what is true, and follow it*. We do not pray that God will be on our side, but that we, *inshallah*, will be on His.

COUNSEL, 52–53

And so We have by Our Command sent inspiration to you:
you did not know what revelation was or what faith was;
but We have made the Qur'an a Light
with which We guide such of Our servants as We will;
and truly you are guiding to the Straight Way, the Way of God
to Whom belongs whatever is in the heavens and whatever is on earth:
witness how all affairs incline towards God!

Knowledge of spiritual realities is a gift, not an acquisition. It cannot be built up out of the words of former teachers, or sages, or even prophets, much less 'figured out' by the human mind working without inspiration from God. No one who lacks the light of knowledge can manufacture it, just as no one who lacks a means of producing fire can light a lantern. But the Qur'an *is* the Light of Knowledge.

The Qur'an guides those whom God wills to guide—those, that is, who want to be guided *on a straight path*. This means that the norms laid down by the Holy Book—both outer and inner, both secret and manifest—are the 'shortest' way from wherever you are now, spiritually speaking, to the Throne of God. The *straight path* represents the greatest economy of motion, where every step, every effort, produces the maximum effect. Those who follow their passions, who seek experience as an end in itself, who travel through life constantly distracted by curiosity, or who stupidly fail to pay attention to the signs of God all around them, are *those who go astray* (Q 1:7). They may be slowly drawing nearer to God, but much of their effort is wasted, and life is too short to waste even a single breath. Or they may we wandering away from God without even knowing it. But those on the *straight path* make the best use of their intelligence, their effort, and their time. From the standpoint of our self-invented opinions about what is best for us, our fantasies of the way we would like the spiritual life to be, the *straight path* may appear to be curving unpredictably. But to walk around the shoulder of a hill is a much 'straighter' way than to tunnel through it with a shovel, even though the tunnel may *literally* travel in a straight line. To follow the shape of the land is a more intelligent and economical use of energy. And it is God, not ourselves, who knows the topography of the country through which we must travel.

To God *belongs whatever is in the heavens and whatever is on earth: all affairs incline towards God.* This means that all things are on the *straight path* already; the return of all things to God is an intrinsic part of their nature, since they have no Reality outside of Him. Nothing happens without God's will; nothing, no matter how far astray it wanders, can wander outside the will of God. But if this is so, then how can the Holy Qur'an differentiate between those who are on the *straight path*, and those who have gone astray? If it is intrinsically impossible for me to leave the *straight path*, then why can't I simply drift through life? The answer is: For those who love God, or reverently fear Him, the straightest path to Him is through submission to His Will, which leads to Paradise; for those who hate Him, the straightest path, immensely longer than that of the lovers, leads through the Fire. So let us choose submission; let us choose *islam.*

COUNSEL, 36–38

Whatever you are given here is for the convenience of this life:
but that which is with God is better and more enduring
for those who have faith and put their trust in their Sustainer;
those who avoid the greater crimes and shameful deeds
and when they are angry, even then forgive;
those who heed their Nurturer (Rabb) and are constant in prayer;
who conduct their affairs by mutual consultation;
and who give out of the sustenance We bestow on them.

Whatever we spend of God's generosity on this life is spent forever. When the goods we purchase—material goods, social goods, psychological goods—are used up, they will never return. But whatever part of that Divine generosity we send before us into the next world will be there waiting for us when we arrive; its value will never diminish; it will never end. So those who are wise investors of the capital God has provided for them will live a 'low overhead life'. They will spend enough on material, social and psychological goods to prevent these areas of life, *inshallah*, from becoming distractions, but everything over and above this they will invest in their eternal destiny.

These verses show us how the goods of time and matter can be invested in the world of Spirit and Eternity, how the perishable can be exchanged for the Imperishable. This material and temporal world tempts us to crime, to shameful deeds, and to anger: resist them, and you are transforming matter and time into an imperishable treasure. This world also brings us opportunities for prayer and remembrance of God, for sharing with our brothers and sisters the labor and struggle of life, and for giving material, psychological and spiritual aid to those who are in need. Time spent in these pursuits is not really 'spent'; it is stored up for us in the vaults of eternity. Every moment of our lives the same choice confronts us: either to sell eternity and buy time, through heedlessness, or to sell time and buy eternity, through Remembrance.

LIGHT, 35–46

God is the Light of the heavens and the earth;
the likeness of His Light is as a niche
wherein is a lamp
(the lamp in a glass,
the glass as it were a glittering star)
kindled from a Blessed Tree,
an olive that is neither of the East nor of the West
whose oil would well nigh shine, even if no fire touched it;
Light upon Light:
(God guides to His Light whom He will.)
(And God strikes similitudes for men,
and God has knowledge of everything.)

If *God is the light of the heavens and the earth*, then every actual light we see, of Sun, Moon or Star, or fire or lantern or incandescent bulb, is a sign of God's Presence, one of the most direct and obvious of all His signs. This does not mean, of course, that when we switch off the light we are banishing the Presence of God; darkness too is a sign of His Presence, though in a different way.

But *earth* in this verse does not refer only to planet earth; the entire physical universe, in one sense, is this 'earth'. Earth is a symbol for matter, the material world. This means that the *heavens* this verse refers to stretch far beyond the material heavens we see above us. When, in *The Opening*, God is named as *Lord of the worlds*, it means that His Lordship is not only over all the planets and stars and galaxies, but over all the universes, visible and invisible. As it says in Qur'an 84:1&19: *When the heavens are split asunder...ye shall journey on from plane to plane.* This means that there are aspects of the Light of God that cannot be seen with physical eyes, but can only be seen with the Eye of the Heart.

What is light? What does it do? Among other things, light shows us the clear shapes of things, and—since there are such things as mirrors—of ourselves too.

Sound comes and goes. Touch informs us about objects, but not about their relationship with each other. But light, and the sense of sight which reveals it to us, shows us the big picture. It shows us things near at hand and things far away. And it shows how things near and distant, things to the right and the left, things above and below, relate to each other. So light is a symbol of a certain kind of knowledge—the knowledge that *synthesizes* other kinds of knowledge into a unified picture that we can understand. It's easy to see, here, why light is a symbol for both the unity of being and the Unity of God. A book or a CD containing images or text may hold a lot of information, but it is only through light that this information reaches us. So light represents a knowledge that is not about any particular thing, but one that makes the understanding of particular things possible. It is a symbol not of this or that object of knowledge, but of Knowledge itself. Light *is* that Knowledge; and, as the Qur'an teaches us in this verse, God is that Light.

The Light of God is compared to *a niche/wherein is a lamp/(the*

lamp in a glass,/the glass as it were a glittering star). This means that
the Light of God does not appear all at once (if it did, it would anni-
hilate us, and the universe as well), but shows Itself on different levels of intensity, which are different levels of being, different levels of
God's creation.

It is natural for us to think of worlds greater than this one as
being above this one. This doesn't mean, of course, that the higher
worlds are in outer space somewhere, that they can be reached via
spaceship. Yet just as the center of the earth below us is a single
point, so the sky above us appears as the open door to infinite space,
filled with the Sun, the Moon, the Stars, and so many other things
we haven't even seen or thought of yet. Gravity pulls us downward
toward that single point beneath us; wonder pulls us upward,
toward worlds we have only dreamed of, or not even imagined. So
our daily experience of living on a planet, held here by gravity but
able to lift our eyes to other worlds, shining with a light we have not
made and cannot destroy, makes the subterranean world below us
the natural symbol of contraction, pressure and stifling heat, and
therefore of hell; the sky above us, the natural symbol of eternity;
and the surface of the earth, the natural symbol of human life, with
both its many opportunities and its necessary limitations, all of
them willed by God, out of His Mercy, only for our good.

But when it comes to our own inner experience, the order of the
higher and lower worlds is perfectly reversed. What appears in the
universe around us as a ladder leading to higher levels of being, in
ourselves appears as a descent into deeper levels of awareness. The
closer we come to the Light of God within us, the closer to God the
world around us appears, until finally even the material world
becomes nothing to us but the many signs of His One Presence.

In terms of the levels of being, then, which are also levels of
awareness, the *wall* in which the *niche* appears is the material world;
the *niche* is the body; the *glass* is the mind or the soul; the *lamp* is
the heart; the *light* of the lamp is the Spirit. The Light of God is an
inner Light, an inner Knowledge, but if we see only by the outer
light, the light *of the earth*, we remain ignorant of this truth. This is
how atheists or materialists look at things. If we see by the inner
Light, however, we will know that the outer light too is part of the

Light of God. This is why Islam does not contradict science. Islam does, however, put science in its rightful place—something that atheistic, materialistic science, acting on its own, can never do.

The glass which holds the lamp is compared to a glittering star. The lamp, and the light itself, are deeper than the star, because they are inside it. The light is Knowledge; the lamp is the human spiritual Heart. So what is the star?

The star is a reflection of that Light of Knowledge in higher worlds than this one. Just as our bodies inhabit this material world, our minds and souls inhabit higher worlds than this material world, worlds which are just as real, or realer, than this one. A great chain of worlds stretches from this world all the way up to the Throne of God, and that star is shining in one of these higher worlds, a world our senses cannot know. Since glass is a material substance, that world is in a way material. But glass, unlike the matter of this earth, is transparent, translucent. It does not block light, but transmits it. So here we begin to get a picture of what higher-than-material worlds are like. In those worlds, what takes the place of the gross matter of this world reveals the Light of Knowledge instead of hiding it. This material world, of course, doesn't completely hide the Light of Knowledge. Sunlight itself would be invisible if it didn't have a material object on which to fall, as well as a material eye to see the object. But in the higher worlds, the Light of Knowledge is not reflected off the surface of objects, but shines *through* them; this is a hint about the quality of Paradise.

The lamp inside the glass which is like a star is *kindled from a Blessed Tree,/ an olive that is neither of the East nor of the West.* What Tree is this?

This Tree is the vertical dimension, the chain of worlds leading from this material world up to the Throne of God. The light itself is eternal; it is kindled by nothing; it is the Light of God Himself. But the lamp, the human spiritual Heart, is only kindled when it becomes conscious of its place in that chain of worlds. That spiritual Heart is the essence of what it is to be human. As soon as we completely realize what it is to be human, the Heart catches fire, and starts to give light. Islam teaches that humanity is both the slave of God and the viceroy of God. We are God's slave because He alone is Reality, while we are merely created; we are God's viceroy because only we, of all creatures on earth, can fully know and consciously serve Him. (The worst thing about modern civilization, based on materialism, is that it has forgotten what a human being actually is.)

To say that this Tree is *neither of the East nor of the West* is to say that it is beyond time. The sun rises in the east; this is a symbol of the beginning of all things, or of any single thing. Likewise it sets in the west; this is a symbol of the end of things. But if the Tree is in neither the east nor the west, it stands above time, or outside it. In time, God's creation begins and must end, otherwise it would rival God, Who alone is the Eternal, Who alone is *owner of the Day of Judgment*. But in God, the perfect idea of His creation never ends; how could God, the Perfect, conceive of something imperfect? The Tree, then, is God's Eternal, Perfect creation; it is the location of Paradise.

And the oil of the Tree is Knowledge. It is liquid Light. Olive oil can be burned in a lamp to give light; it is nourishing to the body; it also softens the skin. Its effect can be felt on all levels: and the same is true of Knowledge. Spiritual knowledge shines by its own light, even if no fire touches it (fire, here, means effort). It is effortlessly what it is. If something is true, it doesn't need to make an effort to become true or stay true; it is simply true in its own nature. So spiritual Knowledge the same thing as Truth as it is in Itself—and God is Truth. On lower levels, we must strike flint or matches to light the lamp of the Heart; effort is always necessary. Likewise oil, as food, needs to be digested and assimilated; this is what knowledge is on the level of the memory and logical thinking. When knowledge reaches the practical level, when it becomes working knowledge, it makes our outer actions flexible; if we can approach and witness situations in the light of Knowledge—a Knowledge that is always exactly what it is, and never other than what it is—rather than in the darkness of raw will-power or blind desire, then we will know exactly what to do and what not to do, in any given situation. This is how the oil of Knowledge *softens the skin*. But Knowledge on its own level simply shines by its own light, which is the *light of the heavens and the earth*, the Light of Allah.

And the Light of Allah is *Light upon Light*. This means that no matter how intense the light we see, material or spiritual, the Light of God is still more brilliant. Our capacity to see the Light of God, and to see by that Light, can always grow, if it is God's Will that it should grow, and if we are willing submit to that Will. But we can never see God's Light as it is in Itself. When we look at the objects around us on a sunny day, we can see that the light of the Sun is an extremely pale shade of yellow. But if we gaze at the Sun itself, we do not see a yellow disk; we see a blue-black one. The sun, here, is a *similitude* of the Light of God. We can see all things by God's Light, and only by that Light can we see them as they really are. But we can't see the Light itself—at least not perfectly. When we look directly at the Light of God as He is in Himself, we are dazzled, just as our physical eye is dazzled when we look at the sun. Yet the fact that the sun dazzles our eyes tells us something concrete about the nature of both our eyes and the sun, just as the fact that God cannot be known directly tells us something concrete about the nature of God, and our own limitations. We are always the servants; He is always the Lord. This is not to say that the Light of God can never appear as an inner or spiritual Light, or that spiritual Knowledge is not possible to us; it is simply to say *Allahu Akbar:* that whatever our level of spiritual Knowledge may be, God alone *is* Knowledge. We know Him in part; He knows us completely. To know this, to be really certain of it, *is* spiritual Knowledge.

Because God's Knowledge is absolutely superior to our knowledge, we cannot reach it by any effort of thought or logic or memory or imagination. *God guides to His Light whom He will;* all our effort—because effort, even though it is never sufficient, is always necessary—must be to ask Him alone for the power to recognize, and follow, His guidance.

And all this, everything that is said here, is only a *similitude*—as is the Qur'an we can read and recite and listen to and memorize and understand with our limited human minds—as is the universe we see around us, and all the other universes we cannot see. God is beyond them all; 'heaven and earth cannot contain Him.' So everything we see and understand of Him is only an 'as it were'. But the very fact that He is incomparable, that He is beyond all the worlds, means that He expresses Himself *through* all the worlds, that every conceivable thing, even something as small as a *gnat*, and as seemingly insignificant, is nothing else than a *similitude* of God, one of His infinite signs. This is how and why He, the Incomparable, may be compared to all things: because He is *the light of the heavens and the earth.*

SMOKE, 39

Verily We created the heavens and the earth with naught but Truth, yet most men know not.

In this verse we can begin to see how dense with meaning the Qur'an is, how packed with Truth. It is miraculous how so much Truth, of such depth, can be expressed in so few words.

What does it mean that God created the heavens and the earth with nothing but Truth? Was Truth a kind of raw material He discovered, or knew about from all eternity, out of which He made all that we see around us, and ourselves as well? Certainly not; to believe this would be to ascribe a partner to God, Who is One without a second. Then what exactly is this *Truth* out of which He created the heavens and the earth?

'Truth' (*al-Haqq*) is one of God's Names, a Name of His Essence. So the Qur'an would seem to be saying that God created the heavens and the earth out of His Own Substance, since there was nothing else beside Him, or other than Him, which He could lay His hands upon when He came to make the universe. But there is a problem with this interpretation too, since it implies that the Universe is either somehow actually God, or else that it is a kind of second God created by the 'first' one, out of His Own Substance. We know of course that the first implication is untrue because *there is nothing to which He may be compared*; we know that the second implication is also untrue because *He neither begets nor is He begotten*. To believe that the Universe is God is the error of pantheism or incarnationism (*hulul*); to believe that God could somehow create a second God is, again, the error of ascribing a partner to God (*shirk*), Who alone is Absolute Truth.

So if the Universe is neither God, nor made out of something different from God, then what is it?

According to the Qur'an (16:40), *Our word to a thing, when we intend it, is only that we say unto it: Be! And it is.* The universe, then, is neither a part of God, nor is it something which exists in its own right, as if it were a second God. It is an *act* of God.

The motion of your hand is not a *part* of you, nor is it a separate object that can exist *apart* from you. Any action you perform depends entirely upon you; any action you perform is perfectly at one with you, with no division; any action you perform, though it is not a part of you, has no existence in itself apart from you. God is the only One Who *is* in His own Nature; all other things only *are* because God Is. Therefore all things, both forms and events, must be acts of God. What else could they be?

This is metaphysical knowledge, the kind of knowledge that the senses and the rational mind alone cannot bring us. But what is the place of such knowledge? What does it mean for our lives, in concrete terms?

If God *created the heavens and the earth with naught but Truth,* then everything is significant. Everything, both within us and in the world around us, is like a word spoken by God. There are no meaningless events, no 'neutral' moments. Everything that happens, everything that is, is like the flow of God's speech, and God does not create the universe in jest; He *means* something by it. This divine speech of existence is not abstract and not only general; it is also directed, *specifically,* to each one of us. Every moment of our lives is an expression of God's Will for us, based on His perfect Knowledge of us.

What would life be like if we could really see this? What if we not only believed, but actually saw, that everything is an act of God?

On the level of *doing,* the knowledge that everything that happens is a word or an act of God is the root of *islam,* submission to God's Will—and the fruit of this submission is peace. This is why all Muslims greet each other in the name of peace.

But this submission is not fatalistic. It is not a hopeless paralysis in the face of events. If we resign ourselves to God's Will, this is not the same as always accepting the *status quo*; our own actions, too, are a response to God's Will (either that, or a flight from it). In the Qur'an, God has given us a mark to meet, which can only be met through effort, through struggling in the way of God; so our effort too is part of God's will. In our submission to God we resign ourselves to events, but we also resign ourselves, so to speak, to our own efforts.

On the level of *knowing*, our understanding that everything is a word or an act of God lets us learn about Who God is from everything that happens, everything that is. Some of God's acts appear to us as events; others appear as *truths*, as things which are always so, no matter what happens or doesn't happen. Whatever happens or doesn't happen, God is all-Merciful; whatever happens or doesn't happen, God is all-Powerful; whatever happens or doesn't happen, God is all-Aware. While we are in this world, all our actions happen in time; they begin and end. But God is beyond happening, beyond time; all His actions occur in eternity. The universe we know is only that tiny part of them which overflows into space and time.

We need to know how to live. And to know how to live, we need to see things truthfully. This was the prayer of the Prophet Muhammad (peace and blessings upon him) 'O God, show me things as they really are.' Beyond the actions the Law requires of us, our knowledge of religion tends to be more or less abstract or theoretical; our practical knowledge comes from our dealings with the world. But if we can truly see how God *created the heavens and the earth with naught but Truth*, then we will also see how there is no theoretical understanding of religion which is not immediately practical, and no practical know-how which does not illustrate some 'theoretical' truth of God. We see ourselves performing actions, we watch things happening to us, and every event and every action—if we only knew—is a Name of God Himself. Work, leisure, sleep, study, driving a car, eating, making love, struggling to change things, accepting things as they are, fasting, prayer, giving alms, breathing air, dying, giving birth, are all signs of eternal realities hidden within the mystery of the One.

FUSILAT, 53

We shall show them Our signs on the horizons and in their souls,
until it is clear to them that it is the Truth.
Doth it not suffice as to thy Lord,
that he is Witness over everything?

When God acts, He does not act only through situations, or only through His speech to us in the secrecy of our souls. He is neither outside us, that He could be identified exclusively with events, nor inside us, that He could be identified exclusively with our own states of consciousness. He is beyond both the inner and the outer worlds; 'heaven and earth cannot contain Him.'

In a way, the inner world of the psyche and the outer world of the earth and the stars mirror each other. Physically we are composed of atoms that were smelted inside stars, most of which have been part of the earth since its creation. On the other hand, our experience of the physical universe is a psychic experience. If there were no conscious soul in us to experience the universe through the windows of the five senses, it would be as if the universe did not exist; even our nightly sleep banishes the entire material cosmos. Both matter and consciousness are inseparable from our experience of the world, and of ourselves as living in this world. There is no matter without consciousness—because the existence of matter could never be known—and no consciousness of this material world without matter, which makes up the objects we see as well as the organs through which we perceive them and the brain which translates this experience of matter into a form that can be known by the psyche. Therefore, neither the psyche nor the world can be the real Source of the other.

Materialists believe that the material world is the source of the psyche. To them, human consciousness is the by-product of matter. If matter is arranged in a certain form, at a certain level of complexity, consciousness is born; no human consciousness of any kind can exist without certain specific modes of functioning of the human brain. Once the brain has decayed, there can be no life after death, no judgment, no paradise, no hell, no jinn, no angels, and certainly no God.

In addition to materialists, there are those who believe that the subjective psyche is the cause of the outer, material world. They believe that mind creates matter. An architect who wants to erect a building first creates an image of it in his mind, then draws up a blueprint, and finally brings together the labor and necessary resources to make his design a reality. In the same way, this group of people—let's call them the 'psychics'—believe that you and I create our own experience, and that you and I, along with all the conscious beings on earth, collectively create the earth, just as an architect designs a building. First we imagine it, then it becomes real.

To some, this seems like a more 'spiritual' conception of how the universe is created. But an architect does not create the laws of physics, chemistry and mechanics he must obey when designing and constructing his building. He does not create the paper on which the blueprint is drawn, nor the capital necessary to fund the project, nor the laborers the project will require, nor the brain which received the first impression of the design. All these had to exist beyond his own will and imagination for his conception to take form *on the horizons*, in outer reality.

Every object in the outer world, every thing, person or situation, the earth below our feet, our society and the natural world around us, the sun, moon, stars, and all the distant galaxies, each one is a sign of God. And everything in our souls, our psyches, every state of consciousness, in all their unfathomable power and depth and complexity, are also signs of God. It is very difficult, however, for us to truly realize this. Most of the time we take our experience of ourselves and the world for granted. We may *believe* that everything on the horizons and in our souls is a sign of God, but we rarely *see* this as actually true in the moment before us. Would we continue to live our lives in heedlessness if we did?

Why do we take everything for granted like this? It is because we have forgotten that God is present in this moment. We do not live in the present experience that everything, ourselves included, is totally dependent upon God. Therefore we are always searching for another cause for the things that happen to us and the objects we see around us. And because we are not consciously standing in *the Light of the heavens and the earth*, this search is mostly unconscious. It is 'natural'—for the heedless—to see the universe as their creator. After all, it is both much bigger than us and far older than us. As we ourselves emerged physically from our mother, so the human race as a whole emerged from the earth, which itself emerged from the universe. This is the unconscious, or half-conscious, origin of materialism.

On the other and, we can act. We can turn our thoughts into articulate speech and move our bodies at will. We can look forward in time and begin to 'take charge of our destiny'. We can make plans, then carry them out. So it is equally 'natural'—if we are heedless of God—to unconsciously believe that we are self-created, or at least to act as if we were.

To believe that we create ourselves because we can move and speak and imagine is to pay attention to ourselves at the expense of our surroundings. We take our cues from our own thoughts and desires and impulses, not from the world around us—much less from God. And so the world becomes obscure to us. We see it as an object outside us, not as a universe that contains us. We act as if we were not really a part of it, through matter, and as if it were not really a part of us, through consciousness. Consequently the world begins to seem like an animal with its own mysterious thoughts and desires and impulses. Here we can see how those who worship themselves instead of God will also to tend to worship *nature* instead of God. They believe in their own self-will; they also believe in the mysterious 'will of the situation' that is always inciting that self-will, yet always thwarting it.

If we find ourselves in this condition of belief (which is actually very common), we need to remember that God shows his signs both on the horizons and in ourselves. God is the Real, and Reality transcends both ourselves and the world—which is why an act of God can sometimes be perceived as a 'wave' which passes equally, and simultaneously, through the world and through the conscious psyche, from a Reality which lies beyond both of them.

World and psyche are equal partners in any event. The materialist may believe that the psyche merely reacts to events; the 'psychic' may believe that the psyche senses events which are to take place in the future, or actually creates these events. But the truth is, only God is the Author of what happens, and the signs He shows appear *both* on the horizons and in our souls. He witnesses both as one in His eternal present; he does not see or act upon one *by means of* the other. (Since we are immersed in time, however, we must often experience His Act as appearing first as an inner state or first as an outer event; this too is in line with His Will, since He wills us, for now, to live in time.) And if prophet or saint knows the future, it is not because he is seeing ahead in time, but because God has taken him, for a moment at least, into His Own eternal present.

As subjective psyches, as separate individual souls, we cannot stand outside the polarity of psyche and world. It is enough for us to know that God can, and does. Only God can know things as they really are, beyond subject/object polarity. And even if a prophet or saint seems to possess some of this ability, he does not do so in his separate individuality. We cannot will to know Reality by our own power; God can and does know Reality because He *is* Reality. He knows Himself *through* us; He also knows Himself *without* us.

THE WINNOWING WINDS, 50

Flee unto God.

The Qur'an urges us to *flee unto God* because God is the ultimate refuge. Whatever winds may blow, whatever earthquakes may shake the bedrock under our feet, God is stronger than any wind and deeper than any rock. His first determination, the first image or echo of His Reality, is Being itself—and whatever *is* by Its own nature cannot not be. It cannot be menaced by the relative non-being we call evil. And the guarantee of His Being is His Absolute Essence, which is beyond even Being.

The command *flee unto God* is addressed to the part of us which is always in flight; it is as if the Qur'an were saying, 'since you are already fleeing, you'd better make the most of it.' At every moment—unless that moment is drowned in the remembrance of God—we are always running toward something, or away from something, or both. What is 'ordinary life' but the endless attempt to avoid this or grasp that, with every breath we take, from birth until death? Whether the good we seek and the evil we flee are of a material or a spiritual nature, the result is the same. The life of the unbeliever, or the still-unbelieving parts of our soul, is nothing but flight, a flight that turns us into chaff, till we are scattered by the winds of life.

But the winds of life are also the winds of God. The very flight we so often find ourselves unable to avoid, or appease, or put to rest, is—if we only knew it—the darker side of Divine Mercy. Our own inability to *be* in any given moment has the potential to teach us that only God *is*. Our scatteredness itself may be, by God's grace, the very thing which reminds us that all things are gathered, as One, in God, and only in God.

We find it hard to approach God, hard to draw near to that over-powering Majesty. Unconsciously stunned by this Majesty, we habitually experience Him as a hidden Reality, as something distant, opaque, abstract. In fact, we find it impossible to approach Him. Who are we to approach the Absolute Itself? How can the finite approach, on its own initiative, the threshold of Infinity? It can do so only by the command of the Absolute and the Infinite Itself. Dragging ourselves through laborious lives, our vital energies scattered, unable to turn toward the *kiblah* of Unity and Life, we are half paralyzed, our spiritual perceptions darkened. Then comes the command: *Flee!* The full terror of our situation hits us all at once— and along with it comes an almost instinctive impulse to turn to God as our only Source of help. So we run to our Sustainer like a soldier to cover under a hail of bullets, like a farmer to higher ground when then dam breaks, like a child to its mother when thunder comes in the night. And what we find there, God willing, will make us thank those very bullets, that very flood, that very thunder. All of them were Mercy—hard Mercy—like the verses of the Qur'an.

THE RANKS, 8–9

They seek to extinguish God's light with their mouths,
but though the unbelievers hate it, God will perfect His light.
He it is who sent his messenger with guidance
and the religion of the Truth.

On the most obvious level, this verse has to do with the power of the religion of the Truth, sent by God through the Prophet Muhammad (peace and blessings upon him) to triumph over all those who would slander it. The word of the Truth has weight; slander, which seems so powerful, is scattered like dust in the face of it.

God's Light has power over vicious slander because His Light is objective. When light arrives, everyone can see what that light reveals, and know that they are looking, from their different points-of-view, at the same real objects. Slander, however, is subjective. It has to do with opinion—with the kind of opinion that does not want to base itself on objective Truth, but shies away from It instead, so that later it can rebel against It. Slander and gossip are an attempt to put opinion on a higher level than objective Truth, as if a mass of subjective beliefs, if they banded together and shared their resources, could finally triumph over Reality itself. But what, exactly, is a *belief*? It is a firm conviction that this or that is *objectively* true. It depends upon objective Reality for any validity it may have. Insofar as it conforms with that Reality it is true, and leads us toward that Reality. Insofar as it departs from that Reality it is false, and leads us away from it. But those who use slander and gossip cannot understand this simple and obvious truth. Because they have been able to reach—temporarily—a false sense of security by telling themselves that this or that is so, and because they have been able to influence the beliefs and actions of others, they start to believe, unconsciously, that they have the power to determine what is real, which is the same thing as saying that they have begun to believe, unconsciously, that they are God.

When God commanded the angels to prostrate themselves before

Adam, Iblis refused. By so doing, he followed his own understanding, based on belief, instead of God's command, based on Reality. He believed he had very good reasons for disobeying God, having foreseen that humanity would wreak havoc on earth, and priding himself on the fact that he was willing to prostrate himself to God alone. In his view, to prostrate himself to Adam would be to ascribe a partner to God, whereas his refusal to do so was nothing but the purest faith in God's Unity. Yet his refusal to obey God's command was itself the act of ascribing a partner to God—Iblis himself. And to place his own idea of faithfulness to God above God's direct command was certainly not a very good example of faithfulness.

Each of us has an Iblis in his or her own soul—or one could say that, as long as our soul is not submitted to God's will, as long as we consult its promptings instead of listening to the word of God, our soul *is* Iblis. This Iblis-soul of ours can construct an entire religion based on personal belief instead of objective Truth, and even call it 'Islam'. But if we follow this 'Islam' we are really making submission, not to God, but to our own desires and passions.

Slander and gossip, then, are forms of idolatry, in which we worship our own beliefs instead of God's Truth. And slander is inseparable from flattery. If we flatter someone, or give undue praise to any thing or any person which does not deserve it—in order to further our own selfish interests, of course—then we automatically slander someone or something else, usually without even realizing it. Listening to the irreverent comedian, and so blinded by laughter; listening to the vain self-important poet, and so blinded by glamour; watching the seductive singing girl, and so blinded by lust, we may not notice the fact that the King has just entered the room, that we are still giggling or making catcalls, when everyone else—even the comedian, the singing girl, the poet—is standing in respectful silence. And to make an idol, through flattery, out of this or that mere human being is also to fail to recognize where virtue, wisdom and sanctity may actually lie, especially if the person possessing them is outwardly undistinguished.

But *God will perfect His light.* Whatever has been hidden in darkness will ultimately be revealed. Whatever has been hidden in our souls, all our vices and all our virtues, will finally appear in the clear light of day: in this life, at the moment of repentance or retribution; in the world to come, at the moment when the souls are weighed and the paths separate, those to the right being admitted to Paradise, those to the left entering into the Fire. *God will perfect His Light.* Truth will prevail. The world, including each one of us, will perform its duty as the mirror of God's Attributes and Names. Submitted to Him, we mirror His Mercy; rebelling against Him, we mirror His wrath; in both mirrors, God witnesses only the perfection of His Light.

God's Light within us is sanctity and wisdom. In light of this Light, all our imperfections will appear in bold relief, either to be repented of, or to be embraced as an effective method (we believe) of extinguishing that Light, there being no better refuge from guilt—until the final reckoning—than guilt itself. Fleeing from God's Light into the arms of guilt, we seek out the company of unbelievers: not only unbelieving individuals, but the various 'unbelievers' within our own soul: our passions, that is, as well as the beliefs we use to rationalize them and the fantasies we use to distract ourselves so that we won't see them as they really are.

It is these beliefs and fantasies, which make up the habitual chatter of our minds (unless we remember God)—it is our own automatic, scattered, reactive thoughts which seek to *extinguish God's light with their mouths.* But that Light will not be extinguished. It will ultimately penetrate every veil that covers It. It will prevail. In view of the fact that this Light will prevail, one way or another, we had best submit to it. And in terms of our quality of consciousness, the way we submit to it is by *listening* instead of *talking to ourselves.* When our whole being rests in a state of listening, we are ready to obey God's commands because we are ready to *hear* them; in the silence of our own wills and beliefs and imaginations, God's Light can fully appear. But if we are always talking to ourselves, then all our theoretical willingness to obey the Sustainer will count for nothing, because we will never hear the Command.

THE CATTLE, 91 (92)

Say Allah, and leave them to their idle prattle.

On the outer level, the Qur'an teaches us here that we cannot over-come the errors or faithlessness of others by threatening them, cajoling them, or arguing with them. Even the Prophet Muhammad (peace and blessings upon him!) could not influence those closest to him if they didn't want to hear; *God guides to His Light whom He will.* The Message is given, and becomes the Criterion; the souls who hear it are either attracted to it or repelled from it, and so it functions also as the Scales. The listeners believe that they are evalu-ating the Message, deciding whether or not they will believe in it. But the truth is, the Message is evaluating them. The Truth, being One, is spoken only once, to every soul, and in that moment, the soul is weighed. This is not to say that preaching should not con-tinue, or that those who have not initially accepted the Message should be rejected, or that those who transgress cannot later repent. But it is to understand that no amount of incremental nagging or wheedling can influence the outcome, which, since it has to do with the eternal destiny of the soul, happens—on one level—in eternity, not in time. In eternity there can be no distinction between God's will in regard to the soul, according to His eternal knowledge of the quality of that soul, and the soul's free choice to avail itself either of God's Mercy or His Wrath. This is the story told in the surah of *The Battlements* (Q 7:172), when God took the seed from the loins of the Children of Adam in pre-eternity, and asked them, *Am I not your Lord?*, to which they answered *Yes, we testify.* In that moment, every soul both *accepted* and *chose* its own destiny, a destiny that no amount of outside influence can change, unless God wills that influence to be effective as part of that destiny.

The Qur'an is also teaching us here that every soul is responsible only for its own deeds and the quality of its own attention, not for the deeds and attention of others. Not every Muslim is called upon to openly and actively preach Islam to others, but every Muslim is called upon to remember God. This is our first responsibility, and our last.

On the inner level, this verse is a clear direction on how we are to practice the Remembrance of God: we are to say *Allah*, the central and comprehensive Name of God, and then leave them—i.e., our *thoughts*—to their *idle prattle*. To do this is to recognize that *all* our thoughts, including meaningless jabber, subtle plotting, hypocritical rationalizations, the virtuous resolve to improve our lives, and the highest philosophical and mystical concepts, are *idle* in the face of God's Name. We should not pay the slightest attention to them— even the attention required for us to try and stop them. These thoughts are nothing but the elements of our own self-concept— which means that, in the face of God, they are nothing whatsoever. To continue to entertain them is like jabbering away in the echoing audience hall where the great King has just assumed His throne. But to try and silence the jabbering of our illusory self-existence on the basis of our own self-will is useless; how can that which has no intrinsic self-existence try, on its own, not to exist? Only the awe of the King's Presence has the power to reduce us to the Silence He both demands and requires. And His Name *is* that Presence.

REPENTANCE, 118

There is no refuge from God, but in Him.

This verse makes it clear that God is inescapable; He is inescapable because He is One. All events, all inner states, are willed by God. It is God's wish that we avail ourselves of His Mercy and avoid His Wrath; the whole of the *shari'ah* has no other purpose than this. Yet if we choose not to grant Him that wish, if we pursue the illusion of autonomy and self-determination outside God, then God's Wrath is His perfect response to that choice. If we show a snarling face to the Mirror, the Mirror will snarl back. We may not recognize the snarl for what it is; we may be so in love with our unlovely demeanor that it seems beautiful to us, as if it were God's reward for our cherished vanity. If so, God may decide to leave us alone with our illusions—and there is no greater misfortune than this. As God says in *The Battlements*, 182–183, *We will draw them on little by little whence they know not . . . assuredly My guile is sure.*

If everything that happens is a part of God's Will, then all the things we pray that God will protect us from are also part of that Will. It is lawful, and part of the virtue of trust, to pray to God for protection; it is not lawful to blame the events and situations we wish to avoid on some power other than God. The *jinn*, the *afrits*, as well as the actions of people who are inimical to us, may be involved in the negative things that happen to us, and in such cases we are called upon to do what we can to protect ourselves. But the *jinn*, the *afrits*, powerful individuals opposed to us, criminal activities, destructive economic forces, disease, social chaos, war and natural disaster are not partners of God in the molding of events, or independent powers which are fundamentally opposed to Him. I may rebel against God, yet everything I do in the course of that rebellion is a perfect and lawful part of the Divine economy. Timur the Lame was an agent of God's Will—like every star and every atom—but this does not mean that he necessarily avoided the Fire.

Those who make themselves agents of God's Wrath, the people to whom God's Wrath is realer than His Mercy, remain under the sign of that Wrath—unless God relents. And those who possess true trust in God will see in *all* events, including the most rigorous, as the mysterious signs of God's Mercy.

The Light of God out of which the universe is made can be compared to the light of the sun, which becomes dimmer and more dispersed the farther it travels from its source. In essence it never stops being sunlight, but its manifestation fades and diminishes as it moves away from that radiant center. In the same way, the Light of God is stronger and more brilliant the closer we are to His Reality. In essence we can never depart from that Reality, since It alone is Real; light is always light; it is never anything else. But in terms of manifestation, we may be relatively far from, or relatively near to, the source of it. To be near to God is Mercy; to be far from Him is Wrath.

It is the passions which experience God's Wrath; fire calls to Fire. And when Wrath comes, we have only two choices. One, based on faith and humility, is to recognize in that Wrath the presence of those things in us which have summoned it, and be sincerely grateful to God for revealing them to us; true remorse is inseparable from gratitude. When someone throws himself on our bed at night and starts beating the mattress, this may not be the assault it appears to be; perhaps a Friend has discovered that we are sleeping with a poisonous snake. Faith can recognize in Wrath the hard edge of Mercy, and thank God for whatever happens, trusting that He knows best.

The other choice, however, is to seek refuge from Wrath in Wrath itself, and this is the quality and definition of all idolatry. How easy it is to make the fatal mistake of seeking refuge from lust in lust, from anger in anger, from cowardice in cowardice. The alcoholic takes refuge from the effects of alcohol in more alcohol; the opium addict turns to opium to save him from the effects of opium.

Idolatry is fundamentally an addiction to an object we pretend can be God for us; and here we can see exactly how an idol is an *inversion* of some aspect of God. The mercy of alcohol or opium is really wrath, whereas the Wrath of God, when it overturns the idols we have set up in our soul, is actually Mercy. It is not really possible to take refuge from heroin in heroin, but it really *is* possible to take refuge from God in God. Wrath is a call to seek Mercy; distance is an invitation to draw near.

Wrath peels us to the core. The seat of God, in our human experience, is in the Heart, the center-point of our psyche which is potentially receptive to the Spirit. When the outer layers of our being start to burn—our anger, our lust, our cowardice, our frivolity, all the passions—our only refuge is the Heart. Who would not take refuge from the sun's punishing heat in the cool shade of the oasis?

If, by God's grace, we can sincerely accept Wrath as one face of Mercy—a face which is perfectly appropriate to our state, the very radical cure we need, and have in fact already asked for—then we can learn to use suffering to feed our remembrance of God instead of distracting us from it. And when suffering itself is experienced as

Mercy, how great that Mercy is! It is truly invulnerable. This realization, of course, is far beyond most of us—except in rare moments—but still, it is a good thing to pray for. We have the right, and sometimes the duty, to pray to God to fulfill our needs and protect us from misfortune; to pretend we don't want these things is nothing but foolish pride. But to see in apparent misfortune only God's Mercy, if we can do so with true sincerity, is a much greater thing: God loves above all others those who can find no fault with Him.

QAF, 16

We (God) are nearer to him (man) than his jugular vein.

From our point of view, we can speak of being nearer to God or farther away from Him. The proximity to God varies with each human being, and with the spiritual state of any single individual. But no matter how far away from Him we may be, He is always near to us.

Some may imagine that to say God is nearer to man than his jugular vein has something to do with gross anatomy—that it refers, perhaps, to the nervous system, the spinal column, which is the physical center or pole of the human body. But this is too literalistic. To say that God is nearer to man that his jugular vein is simply a way of saying that He is closer to you than you are to yourself.

But what does this mean? How can something be closer to me than I am to myself?

To answer this, we have to ask ourselves exactly who this 'self' is. According to the Qur'an (58:3) God is both the *Outwardly Manifest* and the *Inwardly Hidden*. The stars and galaxies do not, of course, 'add up' to God, nor is He the sum of my inner states, or of all the inner states of all the conscious beings in the universe. But behind the veil of outer reality, and beneath the veil of my subjective experiences, God is there. There is nothing we see that is not *essentially* Him, nor is there anyone witnessing this universe *but* Him; He is behind my subjective experience, just as He is behind the mask of outer reality. The universe we experience is not God, because every-thing we experience is limited by our subjectivity, and God is not limited. Nor is our experience itself God; He is beyond anything that can be experienced or known. Nonetheless, He is the ultimate Witness of our experience, as well as the ultimate Object of it. But if this is true, then what is left of what we usually think of as our 'self'? Truly nothing at all is left of it; it is simply a 'place' where God wit-nesses God. On the deepest level, this is what the human being is: the mirror of God. Yet God wills this mirror to exist; out of His Generosity He has given existence to what, on its own, has no right to claim it.

A mirror has no intrinsic shape or color; it takes on the shape and color of whatever it faces. If we face toward the world, we assume the shape of dispersion and multiplicity; if we face toward God, we reflect only Unity—and God, in witnessing us, sees all pos-sible forms and events reflected in us, and knows them as Himself. This act of God witnessing God in us is nearer to us than our bod-ies; it is nearer to us than our souls; its home is the spiritual Heart. The Heart is the place in us where God is nearer to us than we are to ourselves, *nearer than your jugular vein*.

The truths expressed in the verses of the Qur'an are not only doc-trines we are called on to believe or commands and prohibitions we are called on to observe; some are precise methods for contemplat-ing God. Try to imagine a Reality that is closer to you than you are to yourself. What happens? You may begin to have an intuition of such a Reality, but you will quickly find that you can't really imagine It while *you* are still the one doing the imagining; the images we produce through our subjective imaginations are certainly not nearer to us than we are to ourselves. In trying to conceive of God as nearer to us than our jugular vein, we come up against an absolute limit. This limit, however, teaches us something real. As Abu Bakr said, 'to know that God is unknowable is to know God.' We cannot conceive of God—and yet, if He is nearer to us than we are to our-selves, we *can* know that *He conceives of us*. Our knowledge of our-selves is always imperfect, but His knowledge of us does not come up against any kind of limit. So we can say that *His knowledge of us is what we truly are*—which certainly cannot be said about our knowledge of ourselves. In the words of the Prophet Muhammad (peace and blessings upon him), 'Pray to God as if you saw Him, because even if you don't see Him, He sees you.'

THE CHILDREN OF ISRAEL, 81

And say: Truth has come and falsehood has vanished away.
Verily falsehood is ever bound to vanish.

We all know that falsehood has a kind of power. Since it is possible to partly determine a person's actions by lying to him, we sometimes act as if lying were a form of 'creativity' which is validated by being believed. But belief has no enduring power unless it conforms to Reality.

Lying, however, is not the only form of falsehood. Even those who would never tell a deliberate lie often become involved in falsehood by treating an idea or object that is bound to vanish as if it were the Truth itself. There is no more common form of heedlessness than the habit of relying on created forms as if they were God. We rely upon our circumstances, our relationships, our resources, our talents, failing to fully realize that all these exist only as gifts of God. These things are not falsehoods in themselves; the created universe is not literally an illusion. It is our tendency to treat them as realities in their own right which makes them falsehoods to us; if we understood that they have no right to claim the name of the Real, we would recognize them as signs of God's presence.

The vanishing nature of falsehood means that we don't have to spend too much of our energy-of-attention exposing errors and fighting lies, because Truth cuts through error on its own. When our minds are illuminated by Truth, we can see through errors and falsehoods effortlessly. It takes no effort to realize that we have just taken a bite of spoiled meat. We don't stop to analyze it; we simply spit it out. Divine Truth, of course, also manifests as true doctrine, and intellectual errors can certainly be refuted on the basis of such doctrine, which, even though it transcends logic, is always more capable of clear logical expression than error is. But to become involved in fighting falsehood on the basis of *will*, as if the light of the Intellect were not sufficient on its own to dispel the shadows of error, may be to subtly contribute to the growth of further errors. You can't illuminate someone by browbeating him; the sword of intellectual *jihad* is not directed against the moral character of the deluded one, but is used to cut the Truth free from the veils which have obscured it. The grain is beaten to separate the wheat from the chaff; after this is accomplished, there is no reason to run after the chaff, trying to 'refute' it. We simply let the wind carry it away.

It is true, nonetheless, that intellectual falsehood and moral corruption are related. Individuals who believe and teach error are not necessarily corrupt on the personal level; it may simply be the corruption of society which has distorted their ideas and perceptions. But just as every vice will try to justify itself through intellectual falsehood—rationalization, in other words—so every intellectual error will inevitably produce a distortion of human feeling and action.

Error does not exist on the intellectual level alone; it also affects our emotions. If we harbor false beliefs, we will be attracted to things which are not good for us, and repelled by the things we really need. But emotional falsehood cannot simply be dispelled by a better mental understanding. Divine Truth overcomes every kind of falsehood, but this Truth is not only what we usually think of as 'intellectual'; Divine Truth (God in His Name *Al-Haqq*) is also Divine Love (God in His Name *Al-Wadud*), with absolutely no distinction between them. As God says of Moses in the surah *Ta Ha* (Q 20:39), *And I endued thee with love from Me that thou mightest be trained according to My Will* (Pickthall) or *I loaded on thee love from Me,/And to be formed in My sight* (Arberry). God's love comes first because it is intrinsic to His Reality; our love for Him is like a reflection or echo of His love for us. We, as finite beings, do not possess the capacity to love *Al-Wasi*, the Vast; it is only by accepting His Mercy (*Al-Rahman*) and His Compassion (*Al-Rahim*) that we may be said to love Him; our love for Him is the love intrinsic to the His own Nature, appearing in the mirror of the human form.

On the intellectual level, the presence of God overcomes error; on the emotional level, it overcomes *glamour*, which is either the attraction to an intrinsically unworthy object, or an unworthy relationship with an object which requires from us something entirely different than what we are inclined to give. If we are attracted to companions who undermine our character; if we see vices or virtues in other people who do not possess them; if we treat a corrupt man as a teacher or a virtuous woman as a whore, then we are under the power of glamour, in need of emotional purification. We are called upon to overcome the pride and despair (these being two aspects of the same vice) which prohibit us from asking for God's Love and Mercy, telling us that we don't really need them, and which simultaneously portray God as a cruel tyrant Who takes more delight in punishing the wicked than in forgiving the penitent.

Someone tangled in a web of glamour and emotional attachment can only be saved by Truth, and Truth is objective. It is not stuck in the subjective web. It can free us because It Itself is free. Years of struggle to get our ideas in order and to have the 'right' feelings about things, people and situations will only tangle us deeper, unless that Truth dawns upon us. Divine Truth is one with Divine Love, and though this Love is not an emotion, It alone can purify and enlighten the emotions. When our emotions are distorted, our emotional 'taste' becomes jaded; we can swallow the emotional equivalent of a mouthful of spoiled meat and not even notice what we have done. We will derive pleasure from twisted emotions, and feel disgust in the presence of emotional health, of beauty and sincerity, which we think of as 'foolish' or 'naive'. This disgust, however, is a sign that we have been ingesting toxic emotions, and need to be purged. To those in a state of ugliness, beauty acts as an emetic.

Divine Love is ruthlessly objective. It shows us exactly what we should value, what is basically neutral, what is valueless in itself, and what is actively poisonous to us. It throws Its impartial light on the real shape of every situation we encounter; It reorders all our priorities on the basis of Truth Itself. In the presence of Divine Love, we no longer have to work to overcome our vices; they simply lose all their attraction for us. Who wants to eat spoiled meat? In the face of this Love we learn not to give our emotional energy, which is our life's blood, to things which are incapable of receiving it, but to allow whatever is already spoiled to naturally decay and vanish, to let whatever is incapable of living simply die, and give our love instead to the Living, the Eternal.

THE COW, 115

Wheresoe'er ye turn, there is the face of God.

We are always turning. We turn away from this, toward that. Our attention and expectation move from object to object. And since, like the various objects of our attention, God too has a name, we tend to think of Him as an object among others, an object with particular qualities by which we can distinguish Him from the others objects we encounter.

But He is not an object among others. He is not a particular experience, or set of experiences. He cannot be defined as a happening or state of consciousness which has particularly to do with religion, or spirituality, or expansion of consciousness, or deep emotion, or healing, or generosity, or retribution; neither is He a Being Whose particular business is to create such happenings and states to the exclusion of others. Certainly He manifests through these things, but He is not limited to them. 'Each day He undertakes some new work'; every instant He recreates all things in the universe, including you and me. Every state of consciousness, every constellation of events is a unique manifestation of God, never to be repeated. He is the Unique—which is why He manifests Himself directly only through unique forms, events, individuals, and qualities of consciousness. We cannot become familiar with Him through identifying Him with certain abstract qualities we define as 'godlike'. We cannot take Him for granted. His Names are not abstractions, but concrete *instances* of His Absolute Reality. And if we attribute to Him seven dominant qualities, or ninety-nine principal Names, or say that His Mercy takes precedence over His

Wrath, this is not to imprison Him in the things we attribute to Him; it is to recognize that out of the very uniqueness of the unending, concrete instances of His Self-manifestation comes His Awesomeness, His Justice, His Beauty, His Generosity—all the Names by which He names Himself in the Glorious Qur'an. The *qiblah* of the body faces toward Mecca and the Kaaba. The *qiblah* of the Heart—of which the Kaaba is a concrete symbol—faces in every conceivable direction. How can one turn toward the Kaaba when one has already reached it?

To turn away from God, then, is to turn toward God. The *intent* to turn away from God may hide this truth from us, with dire consequences in this world and the next, but this does not alter the fact that whichever direction we face, there is the Face of God. His Unity is too great to be trapped inside our little ideas of that Unity, which are really only partiality. And when we begin to realize this, we may suddenly understand that even God's felt absence is a clear sign of His Presence.

To know that whichever way you turn there is the Face of God is to learn not to resist the turning. In the words of the Prophet, peace and blessings be upon him, 'The hearts of the children of Adam are as if between the two fingers of the Infinitely Compassionate. He turns each however He wishes. O God, O Turner of hearts, turn our hearts toward obedience to You.' It is to be in His hands 'like a corpse in the hands of a washer of the dead.' To submit to fluctuation is to reach stability; nonresistance to fluctuation is the greatest stability conceivable. To submit to change, as God's Will, is to intuit the Reality of the One Who is beyond change. To recognize God's manifestation in the realm of multiplicity is to realize a level of Unity into which multiplicity can never enter.

THE CREATOR, 15

O men! Ye are the poor in relation to God, and God is the Rich,
to whom all praises are due.

God is Rich because He alone possesses true Being. We are poor because, on our own, we possess no Being at all—except His. If we were not poor, His Generosity could not appear in relation to us. So our poverty is really our greatest good fortune.

It is hard for us, however, to accept this good fortune. Though we are already poor in essence, we must become fully conscious of this poverty. We must conform our whole lives to it; otherwise there will be no room in us for God's Mercy and Generosity to operate.

What prevents us from realizing our intrinsic poverty? The barriers to this realization are the fragments of existence which adhere to our nothingness, fragments we have used to build up our ego, our sense of separate existence. These fragments of existence are the impressions of past experiences. Everything that has happened to us since birth goes to make up the sense that we exist in our own right, that we are something other than God's great act of generosity, by which He confers upon non-being the gift of His own Being. This process of making up an ego out of past experiences is inevitable, given the condition of human consciousness in this world; in order for us to function in such a world, this sense of separate existence, this 'second nature,' is in fact necessary. But even though it is necessary, it is still the source of all our suffering, because the picture it gives of ourselves, of the world, and of God, is not true. It is not true because it is based upon heedlessness. Heedlessness is the inability to pay perfect attention, which in turn is based on the inability to perfectly *be*—an inability inherent in our condition as creatures, since only God truly *is*. If we really *knew* that only God is, however, then our consciousness and our being *would* be perfect, because they would be recognized as unique instances of His being and His consciousness. But since we have forgotten this, our past experiences have become stuck to the idea that there is a 'me' outside God for them to stick to—which is why we see everything through the distorting lens of past experiences. We believe we exist as our own experience of ourselves, whereas our true existence is nothing other than God's knowledge of us. We do not see things as they are. God stands ready to write His Name directly on the guarded tablet of our Heart, except for the fact that our soul has already been scribbled over with the half-erased, partly revised jottings of past experience. It's a little like trying to run a computer program on a system where past texts and unrelated commands have not yet been deleted; the result is chaos. In the original Unity of God, when all the Children of Adam who were yet to be born acknowledged Allah as their Lord, the experiencer, the thing experienced, and the experience itself were One. This means that there was no 'unconscious,' no storing up of impressions, no memory. But when the experiencer and the thing experienced are separated, as they were when we came into this world, then experience becomes incomplete. And just as incomplete combustion produces smoke, so incomplete experience produces memory—which is why our direct experience of God, Who in Reality is the only complete experience, is never remembered as a part of our past; the Remembrance of God—and every complete experience is a different aspect of this Remembrance—happens only in the *waqt*, the present spiritual moment.

Incomplete experiences, stored up as memories, are 'repressed'. They drop out of the present moment into what psychologists call the *subconscious* or the *unconscious*—and this unconscious self, this 'soul-inciting-to-evil', is what stands in the way of our ability to stay in the present moment, to complete our experiences in full consciousness, in the Presence of God, and finish with them. Our storehouse of memories and impressions, which goes to make up our sense of separation from God, is the enemy of Remembrance, of the ability to be with God in the present moment, because it knows that once this Remembrance becomes established in us, it will die. But of course it has to die, because it can never really come into existence. It is a mere 'virtual' reality which, in the face of Reality itself, is revealed as nothing whatever.

This unconscious self is what prevents us from realizing our poverty in the presence of the great wealth of the Divine Presence. It does this by appearing to be rich on its own, by seeming to make all its wealth available to us without the necessity of spiritual struggle and self-transcendence. It is seductive; it is easy. The only problem is, all its wealth is counterfeit. The 'richness of experience', the golden memories we savor, all the skills and knowledge we have acquired, are nothing but fool's gold. They may be necessary, some of them, for us to survive and fulfill our duties in this world, but in relation to God's true wealth, they are nothing but poverty. And to recognize this is to become an empty vessel, ready to be filled, out of God's eternal and present generosity, with wealth without end.

THE CLANS, 72

Lo! We offered the trust unto the heavens and the earth and the hills, but they shrank from bearing it and were afraid of it. And man assumed it.

God—Absolute Reality—knows Himself, and the central form of this Self-knowledge is humanity. As He knows Himself in eternity, humanity is His well-guarded secret. As He knows Himself in space and time, humanity is both His slave and His viceroy in this world. The universe is the comprehensive form of God's Self-knowledge in space and time; humanity is the concentrated or synthetic form of this Self-knowledge, because whatever exists in the universe also exists in man.

The burden of being God's Self-knowledge, and thus His representative, was too great for the heavens and the earth to bear. (We can perhaps imagine the Big Bang and the expanding universe as the heavens and the earth and the hills, the elemental energies of the cosmos, fleeing the burden of the trust.) Everything in the heavens and the earth manifests one or more of God's Most Beautiful Names, but only humanity manifests them all; in this we are greater even than the angels. *And when thy Lord said unto the angels: Lo! I am about to place a viceroy in the earth, they said: Wilt thou place therein one who will do harm therein and will shed blood, while we, we hymn Thy praise and sanctify Thee? He said: Surely I know that which ye know not* (Q 2:30). *And when We said unto the angels: Prostrate yourselves before Adam, they fell prostrate* (Q 2:34).

How, then, do we fulfill this trust?

We fulfill it by remembering God—and, on the basis of this Remembrance, by seeing all the forms of the universe around us as signs of God. The hills cannot do this because they are not conscious. The animals cannot do it because each species only experiences itself and sees the world through the single Name of God which is the prototype of that species. The angels in the heavens cannot do it because they see God only as Someone infinitely exalted above the limitations of the material universe and the imperfections of the world of form. Only man can see God both in the exaltation of His Beauty and Majesty, *and* in those very formal limitations and imperfections. So humanity—in potential—knows God, and therefore represents Him, in a deeper way than the angels ever could. God knows something the angels don't know, something which is extremely hard for us to understand as well, even though we are the very subject of that knowledge. He knows how limitation and imperfection, in the context of human consciousness, the human spiritual Heart, themselves make possible His fuller Self-manifestation, a deeper revelation of His Perfection, Beauty and Majesty, than the heavens and the earth and the hills could ever encompass. *Did ye then think that We had created you in jest?* (Q 23:115) He created us for a reason. And when He made us viceroy over the visible world, He knew what He was doing.

THE COW, 31

And He taught Adam all the names. . .

THE COW, 33

He said: O Adam! Inform them [the angels] of their names,
and when he had informed them of their names, He said:
Did I not tell you that I know the secret of the heavens and the earth?

Adam is humanity, and humanity is the secret of God's Self-knowledge, *the secret of the heavens and the earth*. Whatever is to be found
in the heavens and the earth, the names of all things which are also
the Names of God, are all to be found in man. By the matter of our
physical bodies we are mineral. By our unconscious physiological
processes we are vegetable. By our ability to move and feel emotion
and sexually reproduce and respond to the world around us we are
animal. By our ability to reason and choose, we are human. By our
ability to conceive of invisible, celestial realities, we are angelic. And
by our ability—necessarily limited—to conceive of the reality and
nature of God, we participate—indirectly, and as it were by ana-
logy—in God's Divinity, though we do so not by our own exertions,
but by His free gift.

Have you ever noticed how characters like those which belong to
entire animal species, in the case of man seem to belong to single
individuals? We all know people we would describe as peacocks, or
lions, or snakes, or foxes, or gazelles. In our separate individuality
we may be 'dominated' by specific Names of God, something which
is fairly easy to see in the case of the great leader, the great craftsman,
the great athlete, the great physician, the great poet. But in our
intrinsic humanity, we are all of these things. Everything in God is
reflected, in one way or another, in the human state. And because
this is true, by God's generosity, man can potentially know the seeds
or prototypes of things; his art, his science, his philosophy, and his
spiritual realization are clear proofs of this. The angels in this verse
are the intrinsic prototypes or Names of all created things, all things
in the heavens and the earth; and since all things are signs of God,
these Names are both the names of created beings, and the Names of
God which form and animate those beings. The angels are conscious

symbols and living representatives of these Names, but they don't *know* these Names; only Adam, only humanity, can tell the angels their own names.

It is this knowledge which gives man his central and sovereign position in the created order—a power which, when appropriated by the ego, makes man capable of destroying the earth. According to verse 29 of this surah, *He it is Who created for you all that is in the earth.* And if He created it *for* us, He also created it *through* us. Though we were the last to arrive on the earth, we are the reason this earth was made, the seed and prototype of all we see around us. The seed of a plant often reaches maturity just when the plant itself is about to die; yet the seed is the whole reason the plant was born. We know that without earth there would be no man; but the deeper truth is: without man there would be no earth.

THE COW, 152

So remember me, and I will remember you.

AL-HIJR, 9

It is We Who have sent down to thee the Remembrance.

The Qur'an calls upon us to remember God. But how are we to do this? To remember something is to call it to mind, to cause it to take place in our consciousness. But there is no room in our little human minds for the vastness of God. Only the human spiritual Heart has room for Him, and the Heart exists on a deeper level than the work of deliberate, constant and conscious Remembrance we are commanded by the Qur'an to perform.

In verse 151 of *The Cow* it is made clear that the one who gives us the power to remember God is the *messenger . . . who reciteth to you Our revelations* (Q 2:151). So God first remembered us, in our help-

less need, through His revelation to the Prophet, and then commanded us to remember Him, thus making Remembrance
synonymous with gratitude.

According to the second verse, however, it is not God's revelation
of the Qur'an through Muhammad, His messenger (God drown
him in glory and send him peace!) which causes us to remember
Him; rather, the revelation of the Qur'an is the Remembrance itself.
By His own act, He implants the Remembrance of Him in our
Hearts. In the first case, the Remembrance is a response to revelation; in the second, the Remembrance itself *is* the revelation; this
refers, on one level, to an 'infused' Remembrance, a Remembrance
of God placed in our Hearts by the direct action of God Himself.

Remembrance of a distant object takes work; remembrance of an
'object' so overwhelmingly present that It can have no rival is a fore-
gone conclusion. The work of remembering God on the basis of our
own will can never bring us to Him—yet if we fail to remember
Him, what can we expect? We remember Him, and fall infinitely
short of His Reality. He remembers us, and reaches us in a heartbeat,
or even sooner. He was, in fact, already here. Our remembrance of
Him is only an effect of His remembrance of us. And ultimately, we
do not remember God; God remembers Himself within us. In a certain sense, we *are* that Remembrance.